RASH PROMISES

JAMES E SOUTHERN

WESTBOW
PRESS®
A DIVISION OF THOMAS NELSON
& ZONDERVAN

WestBow Press books may be ordered through booksellers or by contacting:

WestBow Press
A Division of Thomas Nelson & Zondervan
1663 Liberty Drive
Bloomington, IN 47403
www.westbowpress.com
844-714-3454

Interior Image Credit:
April Conchie
conchiecreations@gmail.com

Scripture quotations are taken from the Holy Bible, King James Version. (Public Domain)

ISBN: 978-1-6642-9931-3 (sc)
ISBN: 978-1-6642-9932-0 (hc)
ISBN: 978-1-6642-9933-7 (e)

Library of Congress Control Number: 2023908361

Print information available on the last page.

WestBow Press rev. date: 06/21/2023

Rash Promises by James E Southern

Yes, I admit to having made rash promises, and want to express my appreciation for all those who have put up with my brash conduct. Although most of those whom I have offended will never read this note, perhaps it will register in heaven.

CONTENTS

PREFACE

When writing fairy tales, each of my stories began with "Once upon..." In this present venture into Christian nonfiction, I considered beginning "Once, upon a whim, I proposed to a beautiful young lady." But that may not be an appropriate way to begin a Bible study about rash promises.

The study includes illustrations from my life. The aforementioned beautiful young lady accepted my marriage proposal. Thus I found myself committed. Up until that time I had avoided making unnecessary commitments, believing that in that way I would be more free.

Being more or less free to do what I wanted to do, within financial limitations, did not necessarily make me happier. A wholehearted commitment to the Lord would have resulted in more joy. It would have also resulted in more love. Love between marriage partners is amplified by a love for God. Unhappy marriages suggest a lack of love all around.

This is a book about rash promises, not about marriage commitments. Reading about marriage relationships may not help anyway. Many who are miserable in their marriages are also those who have read all the books on how not to be.

This book is for those who have been put off by Christian jargon and pat answers. We all have our faults. Even godly scriptural characters conducted themselves, at times, in an inappropriate manner. Examining rash promises and actions by scriptural characters may help us see similarities in our own lives and acknowledge our shortcomings.

ENDNOTES ON THE PREFACE

The sentence "Many who are miserable in their marriages are also those who have read all the books on how not to be" is not a direct quote. Thus I'm not obliged to get prior permission from Douglas Wilson, the author of *Reforming Marriage–Gospel Living for Couples*. On page 11 of his book, Doug wrote something similar to what I wrote.

CHAPTER 1

PROMISE KEEPING

"I promise before God and these witnesses…
as long as we both shall love."

I f I had ended my marriage vow with *love* rather than the traditional *live*, it might have limited my commitment. Then, if I ever decide to get a divorce, breaking my vow might make me less guilty before God. But I am trying to keep my vow. God is the judge of whether I am more than quarter-heartedly trying to keep my commitment.

A number of brides and grooms pledge "as long as we both shall live." Rampant divorce these days suggests that a large proportion of married couples are breaking their vows. It would be better not to promise anything than to make a rash promise that is later broken.

JERUSALEM

My wife and I got married in the garden of Christ Church in the Old City of Jerusalem. At that time, I was living in the Christian

Quarter of the Old City. (On my first visit to Jerusalem, when the Old City was still under Jordanian control, I stayed in the Muslim Quarter just inside Herod's Gate.) I also lived in East Jerusalem and West Jerusalem.

To tie living in Jerusalem to rash promises, I'll connect one of the places where I lived to the history behind it. I lived for about half a year in Ein Karem, a suburb of Jerusalem. The house I lived in had been vacated by Arab Palestinians fleeing the advancing Jewish Palestinians during the 1948 war. With the establishment of the State of Israel, armies from surrounding countries attacked. Local Arabs were told to vacate their homes for a little while until the Jews were pushed into the sea. That was a rash promise.

In 1966, when I stayed in a room just inside Herod's Gate, I was passing through Jordan on my way to England. I had wanted to go to Israel but didn't have enough money. Those going through the Mandelbaum Gate between East and West Jerusalem got an Israeli stamp in their passports, but with an Israeli stamp, they couldn't enter an Arab country. If I had gone to Israel, the cheapest way to exit would have been to sail to Cyprus and proceed from there.

So I hitchhiked through Jordan to Syria and then, after a side trip to Lebanon, to Turkey. I had to pay my way crossing the Bosporus from Asia to Europe. From the European part of Turkey, I hitchhiked through Bulgaria, Yugoslavia, Austria, Germany, and Belgium. Then I had to pay my way again to cross the Channel from the Continent to England.

BACKGROUND

Although born in Canada, I had lived in England as a child. Thus, having arrived in England, I had travelled around the world. Others didn't seem duly impressed with my accomplishment.

When I was visiting relatives, a cousin who was a curate in the Church of England took me to a Billy Graham crusade. At the end of his message, Billy Graham called for those to come forward who wanted to turn their lives over to Jesus. During the singing of *Just As I Am*, many left their seats and congregated in front of the platform. I wasn't one of them. I wasn't ready to make such a promise.

Before continuing with my testimony, I'll relate my previous experience with reborners–those who are "born again." My reborn friends spoke Christianese. When giving me spiritual advice, they used strange-sounding expressions, sometimes in antiquated English. To be born again, I needed to invite Jesus into my heart. They didn't appreciate my question, "Which ventricle–left or right?"

They didn't answer many of my questions to my satisfaction- questions such as "Did Adam and Eve have belly buttons?" (It could be that they did. When God was baking them, that's where he poked them to see if they were done.)

To me, the story of Adam and Eve seemed like a fairy tale. It might have meant to illustrate cavemen (or cavepersons) beginning to wear clothes. Probably they first wore clothes for warmth, but in tropical climates, it could have been for modesty.

On reading that Adam and Eve, ashamed of their nakedness, sewed fig leaves together to cover their private parts, I wondered what they used as needle and thread. Perhaps they inserted one leaf stem into another, like a daisy chain.

When my reborn friends witnessed to me, I wasn't ready to make a commitment to Jesus, or to anyone. Avoiding commitments didn't make me happier, however. In fact, I was depressed. I even considered ending it all.

"But I haven't seen much of life!" I promised myself that I wouldn't do anything drastic until I had travelled around the world. Then I would decide what to do with my life.

LONDON

My cousin told me of a youth club in London with accommodation for the staff. I went there and told the warden of the clubhouse that my cousin had recommended the youth club. When telling the warden about my cousin, I may have mixed up the terms *curate* and *bishop*.

The warden invited me for lunch with his family and then asked me if I would like to earn my keep by working as a handyman around the clubhouse. Since I was low on funds, I gratefully accepted.

Besides janitorial duties, the job included a wide variety of things, such as stuffing envelopes with the clubhouse newsletter. Prayer requests in one newsletter included "Pray for Jim Southern, our new handyman."

The clubhouse was connected to the Church of England. I went to church and prayer meetings with other young people from the clubhouse and became more and more convinced of my need to be forgiven for my errant ways.

Then one night in prayer, alone in my room, I accepted the Lord. I rationalized that, even if there were other ways, Jesus was the only way for me. Jesus said, "I am the way, the truth, and the life." He went on to say, "No man cometh unto the Father, but by me." Is it possible, then, that a woman might make it by another route?

That night I made a rash promise. Feeling remorse because of having treated a young lady improperly, I promised the Lord to pray for her every day from then on. I haven't kept that promise.

The church that I was attending, and also where I ended up working as assistant verger, followed a liturgical order of service. When the proper time came, most of us would kneel to pray, repeating by rote the prayers in the prayer book.

The wording of the prayers was good, and praying those words was good *if those praying meant what they were saying.* If the prayers were so familiar that they could be repeated while thinking of something else, the prayers could be worse than useless. God doesn't like insincere confessions.

Scripture in the prayer book was in King James English. I had to admit I was wrong when judging my reborn friends for quoting Scripture in King James English. There seems to be divine power in those words, perhaps because of prayers over the centuries that those very words would convince people of their sinfulness and guide them in righteous living.

The year I spent at the church and clubhouse was a memorable year of my life. When I decided to return to Canada, the warden of the clubhouse, knowing my tendency to be critical, warned me, "If you ever find the perfect church, don't join it or you'll spoil it."

BIBLE SCHOOL

Back in Canada, I decided to go to Bible school. The school I chose wasn't perfect, so I could join it without spoiling it.

While a student, I kept the school rules, more or less, such as not associating with the opposite sex unless under supervision. During summer vacations, the school couldn't enforce that rule. However, they did make us pledge not to drink alcohol during our vacation. That was understandable. As students, we needed to uphold the school's standards.

I should have anticipated what was coming. To graduate, we students had to sign a pledge to refrain from drinking alcohol for the rest of our lives. After years of studying, I wasn't about to forego graduation. God knows the extent of my guilt for having broken that promise.

Pointing out that Jesus drank wine didn't seem to make a difference in the school's policy. They wouldn't have appreciated an alternate meaning for the WWJD (What Would Jesus Do) bracelet. It could mean "What Wine Jesus Drank."

Jesus' first miracle was turning water into wine, and he probably drank some himself. Later, he pointed out the inconsistency of the criticisms of the religious leaders of his time. They slurred John the Baptist for *not* feasting and drinking wine, but they also criticized Jesus *because* he feasted and drank wine, calling him gluttonous and a winebibber.

The administration of that Bible school also disapproved of students getting "drunk in the Spirit" and manifesting their condition by "speaking in tongues." They dissuaded a charismatic classmate with whom I hung out from continuing his studies at the school. I didn't manifest such symptoms, but didn't think the condition was all that bad.

There may be a similarity between being under the influence of the Holy Spirit and being under the influence of alcohol. Perhaps it's the lack of inhibition. When Jesus' followers were celebrating Pentecost, and under the influence, some bystanders mockingly said, "These men are full of new wine."

Since that time, I have babbled a bit in private prayer. Could thinking of something else while babbling be similar to thinking of something else while saying prayers by rote?

We do need to think about what we think about. The apostle Paul advised the Philippians to think about things that are true, honest, just, pure, lovely, admirable, excellent, or praiseworthy. This was when he was in prison in Rome. He was probably following his own recommendations, not dwelling on the injustice of his imprisonment.

When thinking of things that are true, it may be beneficial to study the exact meaning of scriptural words. At the Bible school that I attended, Greek was an elective course. A fellow student, when discussing the value of studying Greek, said that he wouldn't study it. He was having enough trouble obeying the English. (He did end up studying Greek after all.)

I took that Greek elective. Thus I could appear knowledgeable, saying that I knew a little Greek. At that time, it was koine Greek which I had some knowledge of. A decade later I could say that I also knew a little modern Greek. On my way to Israel, I ran out of money, so worked in Crete to earn enough to travel on. I learned a few expressions such as *kalimera* (good morning).

Also, living in Israel, I learned a little Hebrew, some of it in language school. I attended *kitah aleph* (grade one) three times, but only completed it the third time. My excuse for dropping out twice is that, as these were evening courses, I had difficulty keeping awake after a long day's work.

Backsliding

I have to admit that I've now forgotten most of the Hebrew and Greek that I learned. Worse than that, I've now forgotten most of the Bible verses in English that I had once memorized. At the Bible school, we memorized Scripture in King James English. Although quoting Scripture to unbelievers in antiquated English may put them off, it is necessary when evangelizing to know Scripture.

I have also forgotten the many promises I must have made during my four years of Bible school. Often, in daily chapel or in Sunday services or during conventions, a speaker would call upon us students to commit ourselves or recommit ourselves to the Lord. The fact that I don't now remember exactly what those commitments entailed suggests that when I was standing up or putting my hand up in response to some appeal, I was making a rash promise.

I've remained a bit cynical. A preacher might say "Let's begin with a word of prayer." I imagine him more accurately saying, "Let's continue with a word or two of prayer, or three or four or more."

I've listened to sermons where the pastor, while preaching, actually *cried*–with tears and affected voice. In my youth, I thought that crying while preaching was out of place. Although I now appreciate the sentiment that prompts tears, someone crying while speaking still makes me feel uncomfortable.

An extended call for a commitment also makes me feel uncomfortable. I seldom respond, as I'm having trouble keeping the commitments that I've already made.

During the extended call, the evangelist might ask for a show of hands of those who want to make a commitment. With every head bowed and every eye closed, he might say, "I see that hand! I see that hand!"

If I were calling for a commitment, I might instruct everyone to put their hands together, and those who want to make a commitment to clasp one of their fingers. Then I would say, "God sees that finger! God sees that finger!"

But I wouldn't say that because of the connotation. I thought of this as a private way of making a commitment so as to foil those who like to count the number of people saved during a particular meeting.

On the other hand, letting others know about the decision keeps people accountable. And fellow believers can be supportive. What Evangelicals call *follow-up* helps keep new converts faithful to their commitment.

Despite my half-hearted commitment, the Lord has been watching over me, enabling me to travel extensively and keeping me safe in some harrowing circumstances. During my quest to learn firsthand about Christian sects, the Lord kept me from being permanently drawn into one. May I be yet more open to the promptings of the Holy Spirit.

ENDNOTES ON CHAPTER 1

Before 1948 all those living in the country that is now Israel called themselves Palestinians. With the establishment of the State of Israel, armies from Egypt, Transjordan, Syria, Lebanon, and Iraq attacked the fledgling state.

The Old City of Jerusalem is divided into the Muslim Quarter, the Christian Quarter, the Armenian Quarter, and the Jewish Quarter. Just north of the western edge of the Old City, was the Mandelbaum Gate, the checkpoint between the Israeli and Jordanian sectors of Jerusalem.

My cousin took me to Billy Graham's Earl's Court Crusade in 1966. Billy Graham called for a commitment during the singing of *Just As I Am*, the hymn by Charlotte Elliot. The first stanza is:

Just as I am, without one plea
But that Thy blood was shed for me
And that Thou bid'st me come to Thee
Oh, Lamb of God, I come, I come

Adam and Eve ate the forbidden fruit, "And the eyes of them both were opened, and they knew that they were naked; and they sewed fig leaves together, and made themselves aprons (Gen. 3:7, KJV, used without permission).

Actually, we do have permission to quote from the King James Version, but not to quote, without permission, more than a few hundred verses from more recent translations.

I like to refer to the King James Version as the Authorized Version as it seems more authentic. Quotes throughout this book are from that version.

In the Church of England, a curate is a priest in training, while a bishop oversees priests. A verger is the church logistics man–the janitor and handyman.

Responding to one of his disciples asking about the way, "Jesus saith unto him, I am the way, the truth, and the life: no man cometh unto the Father, but by me" (John 14:6).

Michael Joseph and Crystal Benson founded the WWJD Bracelet Foundation to release children from poverty in Jesus' name. One hundred percent of proceeds is given to charity.

Jesus turning water into wine is recorded in John 2, verses 1 to 11.

The religious leaders said of Jesus, "Behold, a man gluttonous, and a winebibber" (part of Matt. 11:19 or part of Luke 7:34).

Luke's account of Jesus' followers coming under the influence at Pentecost is in Acts 2. Some onlookers mockingly said, "These men are full of new wine" (part of verse 13).

The apostle Paul's advice about thinking good thoughts is in Philippians 4, verse 8.

CHAPTER 2

RASH WORDS

"Be not rash with thy mouth, and let not thine
heart be hasty to utter any thing before God."

This instruction about not being rash could be paraphrased
"Don't make rash promises, and don't be hasty to utter
anything before God." The Preacher, writing this in the book
of Ecclesiastes, named himself the son of David, king in Jerusalem.
He is assumed to be King Solomon.

When instructing not to make rash promises, the Preacher was
probably thinking primarily of promises or vows to God. These
promises would have been voiced but not because God needs to hear
what people say. God knows our thoughts even before we think them.

Voicing our thoughts, or recording them, helps clarify them.
We have no excuse for forgetting what we have said, whether it's a
promise to God or to another person or to oneself. Even if no one
other than God is listening or seeing what we have written, the fact
that God hears and sees is paramount.

The promises that the Preacher was talking about may have
been made in the hearing of the priests who presided over offerings

to the Lord. The priests usually received a portion of the produce offered, so had a personal interest in whatever was vowed. Breaking a promise to provide food is inconsiderate when people are relying on the provision.

ECCLESIASTES 5, VERSE 2

The quote at the beginning of this chapter is part of verse 2. The Preacher warns, "Think before you speak."

I have a personal example of neglecting to think before speaking. When going through customs at Ben Gurion Airport in Israel, I made a comment, overheard by a customs official, about the slowness of the procedure. At last my turn came for my luggage to be examined. The customs official went through my belongings with a fine-toothed comb. He may have noted the distance between the teeth of my comb.

My combs are often duel–fine toothed on one half and coarse toothed on the other half. He may have questioned me, "Which half do you use?" No, he didn't, but his interrogation was almost that particular.

The twenty-minute examination was when I was *exiting* Israel. Israeli customs examine people exiting as well as entering the land. Besides checking for bombs and weapons, they check to see if people are trying to carry off antiquities.

The second half of verse 2 states the reason for thinking before speaking: "…for God is in heaven, and thou upon earth: therefore let thy words be few." Compared to God, we are limited in understanding. Therefore, we shouldn't be vain, pretending to know it all. We should limit our words.

Applying "let thy words be few" to prayer, we should be precise, keeping to the subject. But praying is not only about expressing oneself well. We need to believe that God does have people's best interest in mind and will respond to sincere praise and earnest requests. Some people speak in what they call "tongues." In this case, it is difficult to tell whether the person is precise and keeping to the subject. The sentiments behind the prayer are important.

Some people when praying seem to be informing God about the situation. They are actually trying to inform fellow pray-ers (those praying). Agreement in prayer does require some knowledge of the situation. In my opinion, it would be better to let others know the details before beginning praying. Of course, when letting others know details, we should avoid gossip.

Thinking of letting our words be few, here is another passing-through-customs story: In the hearing of the customs officer, a child asked, "Mommy, what did Daddy mean when he said 'Act nonchalant'?"

ECCLESIASTES 5, VERSE 1

> *"Keep thy foot when thou goest to the house of God,*
> *and be more ready to hear, than to give the sacrifice*
> *of fools: for they consider not that they do evil."*

"Keep your foot" could be translated as "watch your step." That wasn't a warning to watch where you step while passing the area where animals were sacrificed. Being apprehensive of what was coming, animals may have peed or pooped.

"Keep your foot" was a warning to be cautious rather than hasty. When going to church, we should listen and observe. The word *observe*, as well as meaning to notice or perceive something, means to fulfill or comply with an obligation. We need to both listen to scriptural teaching and comply. Some people, like myself, seem more eager to discuss nuances than to follow scriptural advice.

The sacrifice of fools is probably a promised sacrifice where the promise is not kept, as the context suggests. It may refer to the offering of a defective animal, or the offering of a minimal amount when a person could afford more. It would be insulting these days to put a dime in the offering plate at church when a person could afford $10.

In Scripture, a fool is someone who is not wise. It does not necessarily suggest someone with a low IQ. There are people with a low IQ and a high moral standard who are a valuable part of society. Others, with a high IQ, can be a detriment to society.

A proverb states, "Even a fool, when he holdeth his peace, is counted wise: and he that shutteth his lips is esteemed a man of understanding."

Here is a different slant on remaining silent: "Better to remain silent and be thought a fool than to speak and remove all doubt."

Fools are reluctant to admit making mistakes. "I've never made a mistake. Once I thought I'd made a mistake but later found out that I hadn't." If fools become conscious of their wrongdoing, they are more concerned with what others think of them than what God thinks of them. If their mistakes harm other people, they might feel remorse but they don't realize that they will be judged some day for their *motives*.

ECCLESIASTES 5, VERSE 3

> "For a dream cometh through the multitude of business; and a fool's voice is known by multitude of words."

The Preacher connects fools with dreamers. He continues a few verses further on, "For in the multitude of dreams and many words there are also divers vanities."

Another translation says that much dreaming is meaningless. On the subject of dreaming, the inspiration to write this book came to me in a dream.

In my dream, I was looking at books. A book with the title *Rash Promises* caught my attention. The cover featured a young couple. I woke up picturing the cover with a young couple quarreling. There I was, already planning another book when I hadn't finished the one that I was writing. I have a tendency to start things but not carry them through to completion.

At the time, I was reading a book about prayer and hearing God's voice, so I was practising listening. What might the Lord want me to do?

"Me? Write a book, *Rash Promises*?" I asked, not audibly but in my mind.

"Do you call yourself a writer?" the response seemed to be.

"Yes," I replied. (I don't readily say *sir* or *lord*.)

End of conversation.

Since I did end up writing this book, the dream may not have been meaningless, but there may be vanity in the many words of this book. A lot of it is about me rather than rash promises.

The dreams mentioned in Ecclesiastes chapter 5 may be daydreams. If so, we could reason that, when burdened with a multitude of cares, there is a tendency to daydream about everything proceeding as we would like it to proceed. We might even dream of life proceeding fantastically. However, although we might improve a situation by saying or doing something, we can't really improve on reality.

I admit to daydreaming. As a teenager when missing catching a fly ball, I would dream of being a baseball star. Nowadays, when missing the fly with the fly swatter, I dream of building a fly catching contraption. I did, in fact, build an electric fly-toaster when my son and I were combatting wasps in the attic of our house.

"A fool's voice is known by multitude of words," the Preacher said. Mentally challenged people, like children, need to be encouraged to express themselves. In that case, a multitude of words is not necessarily bad. But "normal" people talking that way would be considered fools.

I have had some contact with mentally challenged people. On

one long bus ride, my seatmate kept talking to me and others around us for at least an hour. Although uncomfortable for me, it was not necessarily bad. Another time, again on a bus, a mentally challenged young man was criticizing a mentally challenged young woman who was also on the bus. That wasn't good.

ECCLESIASTES 5, VERSE 4

> *"When thou vowest a vow unto God, defer not to pay it" (first half of verse 4).*

Procrastination can make a promise rash. It indicates that a person isn't taking the promise seriously. And the longer the delay in fulfilling a promise, the more difficult it is to make the decision to go through with it.

I remember a situation in Israel when I had lent a few shekels to someone who said he was in need. He was delaying paying it back, even after ample money came to him from another source. To give him some credit, he had been speaking English when asking to borrow money. I don't remember if he asked to borrow a few shekels or if he asked if I would lend him the shekels. To us Anglophones, both words imply a future payback.

In Hebrew there are several words used for borrow and lend, and one of the words means both borrow and lend. If he had been speaking Hebrew, he might have said, as translated into English, "Will you gift me...?"

The last half of verse 4 explains why a person shouldn't defer paying a vow: "for he [God] hath no pleasure in fools: pay that which thou hast vowed."

Delayed obedience is disobedience. Moses wrote that being slack to pay a vow is sin. "Thou shalt not slack to pay it [the vow] for...it would be sin in thee." God dislikes sinners or, in other words, fools.

Verse 4 augments the interpretation of the "sacrifice of fools" in verse 1 as being delaying fulfilling a promise, or putting off fulfilling it indefinitely. The predominant reason why a person shouldn't defer paying a vow is that it displeases God. The fact that priests might be inconvenienced is secondary. Those who make rash promises are fools. "Pay up!" The preacher commands.

Sometimes a vow to God might be conditional, with a promise to do something presumed pleasing to God if he would respond favourably to a particular petition. The question then would be if fulfilling the vow should be before God's response or only after God has done his part. And when should God do his part? A person's timing might be within a day or so, but God's timing might be within a thousand years or so.

ECCLESIASTES 5, VERSE 5

"Better is it that thou shouldest not vow, than that thou shouldest vow and not pay."

Vowing and paying what you vowed is good. Not vowing at all and not paying anything is okay, but not necessarily good. However, vowing and not paying is bad.

I remember working for a contractor and not getting paid. His excuse for not paying me was that he didn't get paid. He didn't get paid because the person for whom we did the job considered the job to be unprofessional. True, we weren't professional.

In this case, it may have been better not to have undertaken the job than to fail to live up to expectations. The contractor for whom I was working may have bid lower than a competing contractor. When bidding for a job, a contractor shouldn't promise something that he is unwilling or unable to fulfill.

Ecclesiastes 5, Verse 6

*"Suffer not thy mouth to cause thy flesh to sin;
neither say thou before the angel that it was an error;
wherefore should God be angry at thy voice, and
destroy the work of thine hands?"*

When I first read this passage in the King James Version, I
envisioned a man trying to excuse himself before a towering angel
with sword in hand. (*Angel* is otherwise translated as *messenger.*

This seems to refer to someone sent by the priests to collect what had been promised.)

When the preacher said that God might "destroy the work of thine hands," he probably meant that God might "wipe out everything that you have achieved." People who fail to keep their promises won't prosper indefinitely.

ECCLESIASTES 5, VERSE 7

"In the multitude of dreams and many words there are also divers vanities: but fear thou God."

Divers, with the accent on the last syllable, is an archaic or literary term meaning "of varying types." The preacher is not referring to divers, with the accent on the first syllable, as though divers might be vain.

One of the definitions of vanity is "the quality of being worthless or futile." "Divers vanities," as well as suggesting that the dreamer or speaker or writer might be vain, suggests that the dreams or words carry little or no weight.

I already wrote about the multitude of dreams possibly being either day dreams or night dreams. A multitude of daydreams does suggest vanity, but trying to find significance in many night dreams could be futile. Some dream interpretations could be rash.

The speaking or writing of many excess words suggests the speaker is verbose or the writer is wordy. Talking or texting a lot about trivial subjects is unprofitable. But who decides what is trivial and what is significant?

With people who like to talk a lot, instead of being vain, maybe they feel uneasy in silence. They feel obliged to say something if no one else is saying anything. They should follow the advice, "Don't talk unless you can improve the silence."

Many like to have background noise such as music. At home they might leave a television set on just to alleviate the discomfort of silence. It's not a good sign, however, if a person feels uneasy in silence. Talking, or having background noise, creates an atmosphere of busyness, but it's usually in silence that we can tune in to the Lord.

That last clause of the verse, "fear thou God," could be translated "revere God" or "stand in awe of God." God is far greater than any earthly king or emperor. If we would be careful what we say before a king or emperor, we should be that much more careful what we say before God.

ENDNOTES ON CHAPTER 2

The Preacher advised:

> 1 Keep thy foot when thou goest to the house of God, and be more ready to hear, than to give the sacrifice of fools: for they consider not that they do evil.
>
> 2 Be not rash with thy mouth, and let not thine heart be hasty to utter any thing before God: for God is in heaven, and thou upon earth: therefore let thy words be few.
>
> 3 For a dream cometh through the multitude of business; and a fool's voice is known by multitude of words.
>
> 4 When thou vowest a vow unto God, defer not to pay it; for he hath no pleasure in fools: pay that which thou hast vowed.
>
> 5 Better is it that thou shouldest not vow, than that thou shouldest vow and not pay.
>
> 6 Suffer not thy mouth to cause thy flesh to sin; neither say thou before the angel, that it was an error: wherefore should God be angry at thy voice, and destroy the work of thine hands?
>
> 7 For in the multitude of dreams and many words there are also divers vanities: but fear thou God.
>
> (Eccles. 5:1–7)

The Hebrew word translated as *preacher* could also be translated as *teacher*.

"Even a fool, when he holdeth his peace, is counted wise: and he that shutteth his lips is esteemed a man of understanding" (Prov. 17:28).

Abraham Lincoln said, "Better to remain silent and be thought a fool than to speak and remove all doubt."

The book that I mentioned about listening to God is *Hearing God* by Mark and Patti Virkler. They stress listening as well as talking to God, and paying attention to dreams.

Moses wrote, "When thou shalt vow a vow unto the LORD thy God, thou shalt not slack to pay it: for the LORD thy God will surely require it of thee; and it would be sin in thee" (Deut. 23:21).

"But, beloved, be not ignorant of this one thing, that one day is with the Lord as a thousand years, and a thousand years as one day" (2 Pet. 3:8).

Jorge Luis Borges wrote, "Don't talk unless you can improve the silence."

CHAPTER 3

INSINCERITY

"But I say unto you, that every idle word that men shall speak,
they shall give account thereof in the day of judgment."

J esus was talking to religious people when he said this, warning of
the sin of insincerity. Idle words may not seem so bad, but unlike
idle thoughts that mostly affect the person thinking them, idle
words also affect others.

When saying "every idle word that men shall speak," Jesus wasn't
excluding women. However, idle words for one person might not be
idle for another. For example, a lengthy discussion about whether the
colour of the tea cozy matches the colour of the sugar bowl might be
okay for women but not for men.

The Greek word translated *idle* can mean more than simply
careless. It's the negative of positive attributes such as *profitable*.
Unprofitable words actually detract from any profitable words that
might have been spoken.

I may have spoken a few idle words myself. Being a churchgoer
for many years, I have sung hymns and choruses without really
meaning what I was saying.

LACKLUSTER PRAISING

I just want to praise You
Lift my hands and say, "I love You (Lord)"
You are everything to me
And I exalt your holy name on high

I've sung this chorus without feeling like praising the Lord. While reading the lines of the chorus, I would note the capitalization of the word "You" in the first and second lines but not "your" in the fourth line.

Some people, when praising the Lord, lift their hands high above their heads. When I was singing that chorus, my hands might have been raised half-mast, if at all. My excuse is that I am more reserved because of my British roots.

Saying "I love you" with sincerity is difficult for me as I don't have the emotions that are supposed to be connected with loving. A difficult upbringing may not be a valid excuse for lackluster loving, since love is said to be more a matter of the will than the emotions.

Jesus told his disciples, "If ye love me, keep my commandments." What are Jesus' commandments? Some apply to us believers now as well as to his first disciples. "And he said unto them, 'Go ye into all the world, and preach the gospel to every creature.'"

I've nearly fulfilled the first part of the Great Commission, having travelled to all of the continents except Antarctica. I haven't done much preaching, however. I may yet get the opportunity to preach to the penguins in Antarctica.

Joking aside, there is more to keeping Jesus' commandments than evangelism. He also told his disciples, "This is my commandment, That ye love one another." Love, whether for God or fellow believers, is more than an emotion. It involves action.

Consider the line "You are everything to me." Does that mean literally everything to the exclusion of my wife and son? Hyperbole is acceptable in choruses. Those singing this line are saying that the Lord has a prominent position in their lives. The Lord should have a prominent position in my life, but self is also quite high up there.

When singing "I exalt your holy name on high," I wonder if that name is Jesus or Yeshua. Then I wonder if I'm singing to him or to God. If singing to God, might his name be Jehovah or Yahweh?

Whatever the name might be, when I'm singing, I should be more concerned that God is listening, or both God and Jesus listening, than whether the person beside me is judging my poor singing ability. If I'm singing just because it's the expected thing to do in church, that could be a bit hypocritical.

As well as singing, praying can be insincere. The wording of the prayer might be eloquent, but if the person praying doesn't care that much whether the Lord answers the request, then the prayer may be ineffective. The Lord, however, might still take note of others wholeheartedly agreeing with the person who is praying.

Some say that it is important to end prayers with "In Jesus' name. Amen." Yes, it's important to verbally assert the authority with which we can pray. A phrase like that shouldn't be an add-on indicating the prayer is coming to a close. I remember being criticized as nitpicking when questioning a prayer beginning "Dear Jesus" and ending "In Jesus' name. Amen."

Overfamiliarity

The church I attended in London, England, followed a liturgical order of service. As I mentioned in a previous chapter, most of us would kneel to pray. Having freshly come to know the Lord, I prayed the Lord's Prayer with some sincerity.

There may have been lingering insincerity, however. I had prayed the Lord's Prayer before without attaching much meaning to it. In one of the high schools I attended, the classroom teacher made us recite the Lord's Prayer first thing every morning. That teacher had a good influence on me, but there could be harm in forcing someone to recite a prayer when that person has little interest in doing so.

True, people need to hear the Gospel, but making teenagers go to church, for example, may harden them against it. On the other hand, those continuing to attend church may become so familiar with prayer and doctrine that they think they are saved but actually aren't. This is especially true of children growing up in a Christian family.

Then there are lukewarm Christians who may be churchgoers and may give thanks (say grace) before meals, but in other ways are little different from the society in which they live. They have made only a half-hearted commitment to the Lord.

When it comes to giving thanks before eating, I noted someone's comments after giving thanks. In criticizing him, I'm also pointing a finger at myself as I've given thanks when not really meaning what I was saying.

In the dining hall at Bible school, after getting served, we carried our plates to a table where we sat down. Before eating, we each bowed our heads and said a silent prayer. I observed one young man who had come to the table after I had finished giving thanks. He bowed his head for a short period of time, then began criticizing the food that we had been served.

DISTRACTIONS

When talking about half-hearted commitments, what, if anything, is the other half of the heart committed to? A person half-heartedly committed to something might simply have other commitments such as caring for a family. The apostle Paul, however, refers to family responsibilities as a distraction.

> He that is unmarried careth for the things that belong to the Lord, how he may please the Lord, but he that is married careth for the things that are of the world, how he may please his wife.

Similarly, an unmarried woman can more freely serve the Lord while a married woman has to please her husband. Singles are free to serve the Lord without distraction, the apostle Paul went on to say.

In the Bible school that I attended, men and women sat on separate sides of the classrooms, the dining hall, and everywhere we met together. When discussing this arrangement with a fellow student, I jokingly said that girls were a distraction. After graduation, one of my classmates from the other side told me that she had heard about my comment. There must have been communication between one side and the other that I didn't know about.

There are distractions that are yet worse, such as some forms of entertainment. We may not realize the extent to which we are affected by what we hear and see, but over time our attitude gets adjusted. We might see the "good life" acted out before us in a movie that we are watching, and want to have that same life ourselves. The good life may include scenes of partying, with attractive young people saying or doing things inappropriate for Christians to copy. Exposed to many such scenes, a person's moral standard gets lowered.

A person can also get immune to violence. Although, as a child, I hadn't been exposed to much violence on the screen, I had seen more than my stepfather with whom I was watching a violent scene in a movie. He advised me to look away. I thought he was naive to be bothered by a scene like that.

We also see or read about heroes overcoming adversity and we dream of doing the same. Attaining those dreams, however, may require more effort than we are ready to invest. In my case, failing to become a bestselling author may be due to lack of skill rather than lack of effort.

Gambling or buying lottery tickets doesn't require much effort, but the chance of becoming rich that way is minimal. Lady Luck's promises are deceptive. Then again, the rich are not necessarily *happier*. When I was travelling in third-world countries, provided that people were healthy and their basic needs were met, I saw more happy faces than I see in first-world countries.

SOLICITING

Advertisers try to influence our thinking, persuading us to want something that we previously didn't want that much. Sometimes, after we buy it, the promised level of enjoyment doesn't materialize. And the enjoyment may be only short term. I remember this advertisement for a brand of chocolate: "Go on, spoil yourself!" That's a promise of immediate gratification while minimizing long-term adverse effects.

Often the lure to buy one product rather than another is the fact that one is cheaper. I remember, when working for a church in West Jerusalem, buying supplies in East Jerusalem where things were often cheaper. I bought rolls of toilet paper. I should have compared their weight to standard rolls; those that I bought were considerably lighter. The paper was loosely rolled together. The promised good deal wasn't a good deal after all.

When I was working as assistant gardener at the Garden Tomb in East Jerusalem, the head gardener told me the story behind an unsightly pile of dirty straw. A contractor had told him that he had a load of chicken manure that he was going to dump. The gardener thought the chicken manure would be good for the garden so paid him to bring it to the Garden Tomb instead of dumping it. But it was simply dirty straw, not good fertilizer for the garden.

If not capitalizing on people's wants, it is possible to capitalize on people's fears. Insurance companies promise financial compensation if an adverse event occurs, but they are sometimes reluctant to pay out what they have promised. One of my employers in Jerusalem was in an automobile accident. His insurance company didn't compensate him to the expected extent.

The apostle Peter warned of false teachers making up stories in order to gain support. "And through covetousness shall they with feigned words make merchandise of you."

The apostles were the early missionaries spreading the good news throughout the known world. Missionaries today continue the good work. But sometimes mission societies capitalize on suffering to get the sentimental to send in donations. I'm reminded of a lady receiving a letter from a mission society. Right on the envelope was written "Don't open this if you don't want to read about..." She didn't open the envelope. However, she sent them a donation. I would have opened the letter to see what it was about but wouldn't have sent them a donation.

Thinking of my own form letters–Christmas newsletters that I used to send out each year–I admit to a lack of foresight when making promises. One of my New Year's resolutions was to respond to every letter and card I received. This was decades ago, before email. At the end of the year, I hadn't responded to a form letter asking for a donation, and I hadn't sent one of my Christmas newsletters to an elderly lady from whom I had received a Christmas card the previous year. She had died in the meantime.

GLIB PROMISES

We could get too particular about the accuracy of what we promise. "See you," we might say on parting, but what if the world ends before we see that person again? However, saying "See you, Lord willing" might cause the other person to wonder what we had in mind.

In some cultures, "See you at such and such a time" could be at that time or a couple of hours later. A few months after I moved to Jerusalem, a lady that I knew promised to meet me at Jaffa Gate at a particular time. I got there before the agreed-upon time and began to wait.

It was a nice day and an interesting location so I didn't mind waiting. Actually a few people that I had already come to know passed through the gate during the time that I was waiting. We chatted a bit. I was beginning to feel at home in Jerusalem.

I waited for her for an hour after the agreed-upon time, then gave up. A couple of days later, I met her and asked why she hadn't come. She replied that she had gone to Jaffa Gate, but it was two hours after the time that she had promised to be there.

In the situation where I was waiting at Jaffa Gate, I wasn't inconvenienced that much, but I have disappointed others by my insincere promises. During the time that I spent in India, I felt emotionally as well as physically drained. So many people wanted something from me, not just beggars but even people simply wanting my friendship.

Travelling alone, as was often the case, meant that I interacted with locals more than if I had been with a companion or part of a group. Local young men befriended me. Often, when I moved on, they wanted to exchange postal addresses, making me promise to write to them. I gave them made-up addresses and, needless to say, didn't write to them. It would have been a different story if a pretty young lady had wanted to keep in touch with me.

The fact that I made those insincere promises before my commitment to the Lord is no excuse. Even after accepting the Lord as my Saviour, I have been inconsiderate in my relationships.

HYPOCRISY

Particularly in Israel, Jews watch Christians to see if they act in a truly compassionate manner. They remember that in Nazi Germany, most Christians, if not complicit, looked the other way when Jews were being persecuted.

Unbelievers are watching us Christians now to see if we act according to what we say we believe. The apostle James advised, "Be ye doers of the word, and not hearers only." In other words, we are to live in accordance with what Scripture teaches, not just believe it intellectually.

I tend to be a doer, but not necessarily a "doer of the word." Somewhat like Martha in the scriptural story of Mary and Martha, I attend to things that may not be as important as listening to the Lord. My wife told me that I needed to be more of a be-er than a doer.

Jesus accused some religious leaders of his time of being hypocrites.

> But woe unto you, scribes and Pharisees, hypocrites!
> for ye shut up the kingdom of heaven against men:
> for ye neither go in yourselves, neither suffer ye
> them that are entering to go in.

The archaic meaning of the word *suffer* is *allow*. The religious hypocrites were preventing people from going to heaven.

People sometimes accuse churchgoers of being hypocrites. If such an accusation were made of me, I might divert the conversation by explaining the origin of the word. *Hypocrite* comes from the Greek *hupokrites*, meaning *actor*. Then I might tell about my acting career in Bombay (Mumbai), India. I was a British officer during India's war of independence. In that film, the Indians were good guys and the white men were bad guys.

ENDNOTES ON CHAPTER 3

Jesus' warning about men having to give account of every idle word that they say is recorded in Matthew 12, verse 36.

I Just Want To Praise You was written by Terry MacAlmon.

Jesus told his disciples, "If ye love me, keep my commandments" (John 14:15).
The verse might also be translated "If ye love me, you will keep my commandments." Obedience is the natural consequence of loving Jesus.

Jesus appeared to the eleven disciples, "and he said unto them, 'Go ye into all the world, and preach the gospel to every creature'" (Mark 16:15).

Jesus also told his disciples, "This is my commandment, That ye love one another, as I have loved you" (John 15:12).

The Lord's prayer can be found in Matthew 6 and Luke 11.

The apostle Paul encouraged the Corinthians to serve the Lord without the distraction of family responsibilities. (1 Cor. 7:32–35)

The quote about smooth-talking men taking advantage of believers is the first half of 2 Peter 2, verse 3.

Those interested in learning more about Christians during the Holocaust could watch the short film, *Sing a Little Louder*.

The complete verse about doing as well as believing is "But be ye doers of the word, and not hearers only, deceiving your own selves" (James 1:22).

Luke 10, verses 38 to 42, records Jesus at the home of Martha and Mary. Lazarus, their brother, must have been there too.

Matthew 23, verse 13, is one of the passages where Jesus calls the religious leaders of his time hypocrites. He continues, accusing them of making a convert twice as much a son of hell as themselves (Matt. 23:15).

I was an extra in an Indian film where General Bose was routing British forces. The film may not have made it out of India.

CHAPTER 4

RASH PROMISES IN SCRIPTURE

"Rash words came from Moses' lips."

MOSES

When Moses was leading the people of Israel through the wilderness, they complained of thirst. Moses upbraided them:

> "Hear now, ye rebels; must we fetch you water out of this rock?" And Moses lifted up his hand, and with his rod he smote the rock twice; and the water came out abundantly, and the congregation drank, and their beasts also.

Because Moses had misrepresented him, God punished him by not allowing him to enter the promised land. Although Moses said more or less the same thing about the people of Israel that God had previously said, that was not the time for him to say it. And he wasn't giving God the glory when saying "Must we [Aaron and I] fetch you water."

Esau

Abraham's grandson Esau made a rash promise that has changed the course of history. It made his twin brother Jacob the prominent descendent of Abraham, at least in the eyes of Jews and Bible-believing Christians.

Esau had come home from the countryside famished, finding Jacob cooking some lentil stew. Swearing with an oath, Esau sold his birthright to Jacob for a bowl of the stew. It was just a verbal agreement with probably no one else overhearing it, apart from the Lord.

We in the West who are accustomed to catering to our taste buds might think it ridiculous that Esau sold his birthright for a measly bowl of lentils. However, there must have been other ingredients besides lentils in the stew. At least, there would have been some salt.

JOSHUA

Joshua made a rash promise when leading the Israelites into the Promised Land. The Lord had commanded the Israelites to destroy all the inhabitants of the land that they were to possess. Amongst the people in the land were the Hittites, and one of the clans of the Hittites were the Gibeonites. The Gibeonites, hearing what the Israelites had done to Jericho and Ai, sent a delegation to make a treaty with the Israelites. They pretended to have come from a distant land where the Israelites were under no obligation to destroy the inhabitants.

Joshua promised to let the Gibeonites live. It was just his word given to a delegation of the Gibeonites, but that was sufficient in those days. The Gibeonites relied on the Israelites to honour the treaty. Even a promise made in error needed to be kept.

When the Israelites found out they had been deceived, they dared not break their oath to the Gibeonites, fearing God's wrath on covenant breakers. Instead of killing them, the Israelites subjected them to servitude, making them cutters of wood and drawers of water. From the Gibeonites' point of view, this was a better outcome.

Cutting wood reminds me of an incident when I was living in Ein Karem near the Jerusalem Forest. There are a number of churches in Ein Karem as that was the birthplace of John the Baptist.

I was working for an Israeli who considered Saturday to be the day of rest and Sunday to be the first work day of the week. One Sunday morning he sent me out to saw firewood from a broken-down tree. This was before I became involved with church work so I wasn't even thinking of Sunday being a day of worship.

Just as I was finishing, having shut off the chainsaw, I noticed some men passing by scowling at me. One of them wore a cleric's garb. They were from the nearby church. In Ein Karem, sawing on Sunday is rather rash.

JEPHTHAH

One of Israel's judges made a rash promise. Jephthah was about to lead the Israelites in a battle against the Ammonites. If the Lord gave him victory, he vowed to sacrifice as a burnt offering to the Lord whatever came out the door of his house to meet him when he returned in triumph.

The Israelites defeated the Ammonites. When Jephthah returned, his only child, a daughter, came out to meet him, dancing to the sound of tambourines. Jephthah was distressed, but because he wouldn't break his promise, he did sacrifice her.

What else might have come out of the door of his house? A house pet? Dogs would have lived mostly outside and, anyway, a dog wouldn't have been acceptable as a sacrifice. Some homes were a combined home and barn. Perhaps goats strolled in and out through the door.

The other day when I was buying free-range eggs at a local farm, a hen went in the door of the house as my eggs were being handed to me outside. I doubt that it laid its eggs in the house. It probably would have been redirected to the chicken coop after I left.

KING SAUL

Israel's first king, Saul, was also prone to rash promises. The Israelites were battling the Philistines and Saul had bound the Israelites under an oath, "Cursed be any man who eats food before evening comes, before I avenge myself on my enemies."

So none of the troops ate anything, thus having less strength for the battle. They still won, but by the end of the day they were exhausted. When asking the Lord if they should pursue the Philistines that night, Saul deduced that some sin had been committed. He promised, "As surely as the Lord who rescues Israel lives, even if it lies with my son Jonathan, he must die."

Saul's son, Jonathan, hadn't heard of his father's curse on anyone who ate something. He confessed that he had eaten some honey but objected to being killed.

"And Saul answered, 'God do so and more also; for thou shalt surely die, Jonathan.'"

"God do so and more also" was Saul saying that God should kill him if he did not have Jonathan killed. But the men prevented Saul from keeping his promise. They reminded him that Jonathan had instigated their victory over the Philistines.

King Saul had asked God to kill him if Jonathan was not killed. Years later, when the time came, King Saul helped God kill him by falling on his own sword.

SHIMEI

A few decades after King Saul, Shimei made a rash promise to King Solomon. The story begins with Solomon's father, David, fleeing from his son Absalom. Shimei cursed him. When David returned in victory, Shimei met him and pleaded for forgiveness. Some wanted to kill Shimei for having cursed the Lord's anointed, but David wouldn't let them. He promised Shemei with an oath that he wouldn't allow them to kill him.

However, on his deathbed, David made Solomon promise to arrange a bloody death for Shimei. So, Solomon summoned him and invited him to come and live in Jerusalem. But once coming to Jerusalem, he was never to leave, on pain of death. Shimei promised, "The saying is good; as my lord the king hath said, so will thy servant do."

But three years later Shimei visited Gath. On hearing about it, Solomon summoned Shimei and asked, "Why then hast thou not kept the oath of the LORD, and the commandment that I have charged thee with?"

Then, at Solomon's command, Shimei was executed.

Gath was probably located in what is now the Gaza Strip. When I lived in Jerusalem, I visited some Israeli settlements there. Some people believe Prime Minister Ariel Sharon made a rash decision when disengaging from the Gaza Strip. It didn't result in peace.

KING SOLOMON

It seems that Solomon himself didn't keep a promise to his mother. She had come to him with "one small request."

Solomon replied, "Ask on, my mother: for I will not say thee nay."

His mother then asked permission for Solomon's half-brother Adonijah to marry Abishag, King David's young attendant. Upon hearing this, Solomon realized that granting the request would be a threat to his rule. He refused and ordered that Adonijah be killed.

King Solomon may have kept his promises to his brides, if grooms in those days did make promises. His promise to his seven-hundredth wife might have been "I promise to love you no less than my other wives."

KING AHAB

Ahab, an ungodly king of Israel, made a treaty with Benhadad, king of Syria, after he and his army had defeated the Syrians. Benhadad had come out of hiding to plead for a truce, promising that the Israelite cities previously taken by the Syrians would be returned. And Ahab would be given trading rights in Damascus.

Then Ahab promised, "I will send thee away with this covenant."

He made a treaty with Benhadad and sent him away. However, the Lord did not want him to let Benhadad go.

A prophet told Ahab, "Thus saith the LORD, Because thou hast let go out of thy hand a man whom I appointed to utter destruction, therefore thy life shall go for his life, and thy people for his people." Ahab was later killed in battle with the Syrians.

KING ZEDEKIAH

Zedekiah, the last king of Judah, didn't keep his promise to Nebuchadnezzar of Babylon who had subjugated Judah. Zedekiah "rebelled against king Nebuchadnezzar who had made him swear by God." Zedekiah had sworn allegiance to Nebuchadnezzar.

God could not condone rebelling after swearing allegiance. When the Babylonians broke through the walls of Jerusalem, Zedekiah tried to flee but was captured. As punishment, Nebuchadnezzar ordered that Zedekiah's sons be killed before his eyes. Then they put out his eyes, bound him with shackles and took him to Babylon to add to Nebuchadnezzar's king collection.

KING ANTIOCHUS

Adding another example of a broken promise to this section about scriptural stories means defining Scripture. As teenagers, my reborn friends and I discussed the meaning of Scripture. They referred to the King James Version of the Bible as Scripture.

I have since learned that the original 1611 King James Version included books that are now considered apocryphal. Just to be provocative, I'm including a story from 1 Maccabees.

Judas Maccabeus and his brothers lived during the second century BC when Judea was part of the Greek Seleucid Empire. The brothers led armed resistance against those promoting the Hellenization of Judea.

Judas and his troops had retreated when fighting a vast army of young King Antiochus the Fifth. The king then marched up to Jerusalem and besieged it, but because there was a threat to his kingdom, he decided to make peace with the Jews and withdraw. When he solemnly agreed to allow the Jews to follow their own laws and customs, they came out of their fortress.

"Then the king entered into mount Sion, but when he saw the strength of the place, he broke his oath that he had made, and gave commandment to pull down the wall round about." ("Mount Sion" refers to a fortress that either was the walled city of Jerusalem or was part of the city.)

KING HEROD

A couple of centuries later, the Romans were ruling over the Jews. Although the Romans recognized Judaism as a valid religion, they championed Greek permissiveness. Herod Antipas, who sympathized with the Romans, imprisoned John the Baptist because John had criticized his marriage to Herodias, his brother's wife.

During a banquet on Herod's birthday, Herodias' daughter danced before him and his guests. She pleased him so much that he promised, "Ask of me whatsoever thou wilt, and I will give it thee." And he swore, "Whatsoever thou shalt ask of me, I will give it thee, unto the half of my kingdom."

After consulting with her mother, she asked for John the Baptist's head on a platter. Because of his vow in front of his guests, Herod reluctantly gave the order. John was beheaded and his head brought on a platter and given to the girl.

If a promise of "unto the half of my kingdom" had been made to me, I might have first determined if "unto" meant "up to" or "up to and including." Then I might have asked for five twelfths of his kingdom or the whole half. Actually, vowing extravagant amounts like that was not taken too literally.

Peter

When promising something, a person might sincerely believe he will keep his promise, not realizing his own weakness. However, because of fear or some such emotion, he breaks his promise.

When Jesus told his disciples that he was going to be betrayed and that they would all fall away, Peter promised, "Though all men shall be offended because of thee, yet will I never be offended." He repeated his promise, "Though I should die with thee, yet will I not deny thee."

When Peter was in the courtyard of the high priest after Jesus was arrested, he denied three times that he knew Jesus. When accused of being seen with Jesus, he said, "I know not what thou sayest." And again he denied with an oath, "I do not know the man." They accused him again. Then he began to curse and to swear, saying "I know not the man."

Later, Peter was truly repentant. Trustfully, Jesus annulled the curse that Peter had pronounced upon himself.

We shouldn't single out Peter and his rash promise never to deny Jesus. The other disciples vowed the same. And by calling the promise "rash," it doesn't mean that it was a bad promise to make. But the disciples didn't realize their own timidity in the face of seemingly overpowering evil.

Ananias and Sapphira

With the establishment of the church in Jerusalem, Peter became a leader. There is an account of him dealing with a couple of hypocrites.

> A certain man named Ananias, with Sapphira his wife, sold a possession, and kept back part of the price, his wife also being privy to it, and brought a certain part, and laid it at the apostles' feet. But Peter said, "Ananias, why hath Satan filled thine heart to

lie to the Holy Ghost, and to keep back part of the price of the land? Whiles it remained, was it not thine own? and after it was sold, was it not in thine own power?"

God struck them both dead.

Forty Jews

When the apostle Paul was imprisoned in Jerusalem, more than forty Jews went to the chief priests and elders saying that they had bound themselves under a great curse that they would eat nothing until they had slain Paul. They wanted the chief priests and elders to ask the commander to bring Paul back to the Sanhedrin, planning an ambush to kill him on the way. Paul's nephew, however, heard of the plot and warned the commander,

> Do not thou yield unto them, for there lie in wait for him of them more than forty men which have bound themselves with an oath that they will neither eat nor drink till they have killed him, and now are they ready, looking for a promise from thee.

So the commander sent Paul to Caesarea out of harm's way.

Two years later the chief priests and Jewish leaders in Jerusalem were trying to convince Governor Festus to transfer Paul to Jerusalem, plotting to kill him on the way. If any of the original more than forty men were among those in this second plot, they must have been quite hungry.

ENDNOTES ON CHAPTER 4

"Rash words came from Moses' lips" is part of Psalm 106, verse 33. In the King James Version, it reads: "He [Moses] spake unadvisedly with his lips."

The passage where Moses brings water out of a rock is in Numbers 20. The quote is part of verses 10 and 11.

The account of Esau swearing an oath to sell Jacob his birthright is in Genesis 25, verses 29 to 34.

The account of Joshua making a covenant with the Gibeonites is in Joshua 9.

Moses' warning not to make a covenant with the people of the land can be found in Exodus 34, verse 12. "Take heed to thyself, lest thou make a covenant with the inhabitants of the land whither thou goest, lest it be for a snare in the midst of thee."

See also Deuteronomy 7, verses 1 and 2.

The account of Jephthah vowing to make a sacrifice to the Lord and then having to sacrifice his own daughter is found in Judges 11, verses 30 to 39. Some theologians believe that Jephthah merely dedicated his daughter in service at the tabernacle, so she remained a virgin for the rest of her life.

The account of Israel routing the Philistines and Saul's rash promises is in 1 Samuel 14. Saul's curse on anyone eating food before sunset is in verse 24. Saul swearing that the guilty man should die is in verse 39. Saul pronouncing a curse upon himself if Jonathan was not punished is in verse 44.

1 Samuel 31 records the Philistines routing Israel and King Saul killing himself rather than being mistreated by the Philistines.

Shimei cursed King David (2 Sam. 16:5–13); Shimei asked for forgiveness (2 Sam. 19:18–23); David instructed Solomon regarding Shimei (1 Kings 2:8–9); Solomon dealt with Shimei (1 Kings 2:36–46).

The story of King Solomon's mother requesting that he grant her one small favour and King Solomon's response is in 1 Kings 2, verses 13 to 25. The quote is part of verse 20.

The account of King Ahab sparing King Benhadad of Syria (Aram) is in 1 Kings 20, verses 31 to 34. The quote where King Ahab promised to let King Benhadad go is part of verse 34. The quote where the prophet condemns King Ahab for his rash promise is part of a subsequent verse, verse 42.

The account of King Ahab dying in battle against the Syrians is in 1 Kings 22, verses 29 to 38.

Zedekiah did not humble himself before Jeremiah the prophet. "And he also rebelled against king Nebuchadnezzar, who had made him swear by God: but he stiffened his neck, and hardened his heart from turning unto the LORD God of Israel" (2 Chron. 36:13).

The account of Zedekiah's capture, his sons being killed before his eyes, and then his eyes being put out is in 2 Kings 25.

The account of King Antiochus the Fifth besieging Jerusalem is in 1 Maccabees 6. Verse 62 is quoted in the King James Version.

1 Maccabees is one of several apocryphal books that were published in the original King James Bible. According to the King James Bible Online, the Apocrypha was a part of the KJV until it was removed in 1885.

Herod's rash promise to Herodias' daughter is found in Matthew 14 as well as Mark 6. The quotes are parts of Mark 6, verses 22 and 23.

The reason that John the Baptist criticized Herod was that marriage to a brother's wife while the brother was still living was forbidden by Mosaic Law. (See Lev. 20:31.) Herod had married

Herodias, the former wife of his half-brother Philip. And Herod's divorced wife had married Philip. It was a case of wife swapping.

Peter's promise not to deny Jesus is recorded in three of the Gospels, and his denial in all four. The quotes are from Matthew 26, parts of verses 33, 35, 70, 72, and 74.

The account of Ananias and Sapphira is in Acts 5, verses 1 to 11. The quotes are verses 1 to 3 and part of verse 4.

The account of more than forty Jews vowing not to eat anything until they had killed Paul is found in Acts 23. The quote where Paul's nephew talks to the commander is verse 21. He said that they had promised not to drink as well as not to eat anything. Verse 12 also mentions *drink* as well as *eat*.

As an aside, what Paul's nephew said to the commander illustrates the difference between a promise and an oath. The oath of the more than forty men was more binding than the promise that the commander might have made. The King James Version has the Jews "looking for a promise from thee [from the commander]." Another translation is "waiting for your consent to their request."

CHAPTER 5

FAMILY STORIES

The story behind the cover image

JOE AND JODY

Joe came from a family where the women of the household washed the dishes. Jody came from a family where the men of the household washed the dishes. When Joe and Jody got married, neither of them was willing to adjust. Consequently, dirty dishes, cups and cutlery built up in the kitchen sink, beside the kitchen sink and on the kitchen counters.

They ended up eating mostly pizzas–anything that could be eaten with the fingers. There would have been the option of paper plates and plastic cutlery but Jody disliked the idea of creating so much waste.

They also made sandwiches. The butter knife was left in the butter and Jody made Joe promise not to use it for anything else. The story continues:

Jody: There's peanut butter on the butter knife!

Joe: Where? (He thought he had wiped it all off on the bread.)

She showed him.

Joe: Well, peanut butter is butter.

Jody: You knew what I meant when I said not to use the knife for anything but the butter.

Joe: Did you say "but the butter" or simply "but butter"?

Jody: You broke your promise. Admit it!

Joe: You're overly fussy.

Jody: Promise breaker!

Joe: Fusspot!

Jody: Promise breaker!

The front cover depicts Joe explaining to Jody that it makes a difference whether a person uses the word *the*.

Here are some family stories, inspired by reflection on my childhood and my fatherhood:

CAMPING

A man was camping with his wife and son, and promised to prepare breakfast the next morning. However, the next morning was rainy. He decided to prepare breakfast *under* the picnic table where it was somewhat sheltered.

Preparing to cook an omelet took more time than he had calculated as he had broken the eggs directly into the frying pan rather than dirtying a bowl. Stirring the eggs and other ingredients took time as he had to be careful not to slop it over the edge of the pan. Also, it was uncomfortable squatting under the table. By the time he had the frying pan on top of the camp stove and was ready to light the stove, it had stopped raining. Thus it would be better to cook the omelet on the table rather than under the table.

He was shifting position in order to get out from under the table when he heard "What on earth are you doing under there!" It was his wife. Startled, he lost his balance and put his hand down to steady himself. Unfortunately, he put his hand down on the handle of the frying pan and it flipped up, throwing its contents over him.

Egg on his face was all because of a rash promise.

FATHER AND SON

A father was talking to his young son.

Dad: You've been eating chocolate.
Son: How do you know?
Dad: A little bird told me.
Son: Birds can't talk!
Dad: Some parrots can.
Son: English?
Dad: Pigeon English or, rather, parrot English. Actually, parrots only parrot words, but don't understand what they're saying.
Son: What did you mean when you said that a little bird told you?

Dad:	It means that you've been found out.
Son:	How did you find out?
Dad:	You have chocolate on your face. Does Mom know you ate the chocolate?
Son:	I don't think so.
Dad:	Didn't you promise to ask first?
Son:	I forgot.
Dad:	You need to keep your promises.

A father was explaining to his young son what was meant by the expression "Good Samaritan." It refers to a compassionate person–someone who helps another in need, with no thought of reward for offering a helping hand.

The expression comes from one of Jesus' parables. A man from Samaria helped an injured Jew. The Samaritan took him to an inn and paid for his stay there. He promised the innkeeper that if more expenses were incurred, he would repay him when he returned.

Son:	What if the Good Samaritan didn't return to the inn? Might he have left his phone number with the innkeeper?
Dad:	They didn't have phones in those days.
Son:	Did they send letters back and forth?
Dad:	No postal service, as far as I know.
Son:	Might the Good Samaritan have left something with the innkeeper, like a watch, that he could sell if the Good Samaritan didn't return?
Dad:	They didn't have watches in those days.
Son:	How did they tell time?
Dad:	Sundials.
Son:	Might he have left his sundial with him?
Dad:	Portable sundials don't work.
Son:	Why not?
Dad:	Listen. The innkeeper probably didn't ask for anything as a pledge of payment. He trusted that the Good Samaritan was not making a rash promise.

A father and son were reading one of Jesus' parables.

The kingdom of heaven is likened unto a certain king, which would take account of his servants.

And when he had begun to reckon, one was brought unto him, which owed him ten thousand talents.

But forasmuch as he had not to pay, his lord commanded him to be sold, and his wife, and children, and all that he had, and payment to be made.

The servant therefore fell down, and worshipped him, saying, Lord, have patience with me, and I will pay thee all.

Then the lord of that servant was moved with compassion, and loosed him, and forgave him the debt.

But the same servant went out, and found one of his fellowservants, which owed him an hundred pence: and he laid hands on him, and took him by the throat, saying, Pay me that thou owest.

And his fellowservant fell down at his feet, and besought him, saying, Have patience with me, and I will pay thee all.

And he would not: but went and cast him into prison, till he should pay the debt.

So when his fellowservants saw what was done, they were very sorry, and came and told unto their lord all that was done.

Then his lord, after that he had called him, said unto him, O thou wicked servant, I forgave thee all that debt, because thou desiredst me:

Shouldest not thou also have had compassion on thy fellowservant, even as I had pity on thee?

And his lord was wroth, and delivered him to the tormentors, till he should pay all that was due unto him.

Son:	How much is ten thousand talents?
Dad:	The equivalent of millions of dollars today, maybe billions tomorrow at the present rate of inflation.
Son:	So the king ordered that he be sold as a slave?
Dad:	Yes, he and his family.
Son:	Would his sons have been valued more than his daughters?
Dad:	I don't know, but he begged the king to be patient and he would pay it all. So the king forgave him.
Son:	Would the guy have been able to pay millions of dollars?
Dad:	That does seem like a rash promise. He tried to collect a debt of a few thousand dollars that another servant owed him.
Son:	So he had the guy thrown in prison until he paid up. Might he have had to work in a chain gang?
Dad:	Those Roman roads must have required a few work crews.
Son:	What if he were chained together with other prisoners and needed to go to the toilet?
Dad:	Let's not go there. Other servants were upset and told the king that the servant had thrown his fellow servant into prison.
Son:	Tattle tales!
Dad:	The king reprimanded him, saying that he should have had mercy on his fellow servant as he, the king, had mercy on him.
Son:	And the king sent him to the torturers until he paid up. But how could he pay anything while he was strung up by his thumbs?
Dad:	The parable is an allegory, like he was sent to hell.
Son:	Like forever?
Dad:	It's difficult to imagine what it would be like outside of space-time.
Son:	Mom might not be telling me it's time to go to bed.

Jonny Stories

Jonny promised to himself never again to eat turnip. This was when his mom made him finish eating the turnip on his plate. Subsequently, his mom allowed him to serve himself, but he had to take some of all the food on the table. When his mom served turnip, he would touch the serving spoon to his plate, leaving just a smear of turnip. He had difficulty disposing of that smear without his mom seeing what he was doing.

Jonny's mom had promised that he could serve himself as much as he wanted or as little as he wanted of everything she set on the table. She had to revise her promise to say that "as little" did not include zero.

She also had to revise her promise to say that "as much as he wanted" was only after others had helped themselves. This was after she had put an apple pie on the table.

Jonny's mom stipulated that those leaving the dinner table needed to ask to be excused. That expanded to include the breakfast and lunch table as well. The rule changed to only the first person leaving the table needing to ask to be excused. Jonny had caught his mom failing to ask to be excused. She was the last person leaving the table.

Later, when Jonny was a teenager, his mom allowed him to prepare food for himself, but he had to wash his own dishes. She had to revise her directives to include washing, as well as dishes, any cups, cutlery, pots, or pans that he used. And they needed to be washed that same day.

In Jonny's preteen years, his mom promised not to make him have a haircut until his hair hung over his eyes. So Jonny regularly combed his hair forward and trimmed it just above the eyes.

Jonny promised not to shoot arrows in the house. He had received a set of bow and arrows as a birthday present. He was just testing it out, pulling back the string of the bow with an arrow in place. Unfortunately, however, the string slipped out from between his fingers.

Jonny promised to take care of Miss Piggy, the guinea pig, if his mom kept it. His mom had planned to give Miss Piggy away for safe-keeping. Their dog, Jack, had finished off the other guinea pigs, thinking they were rats. Jonny persuaded his mom to keep Miss Piggy. After a few weeks of his mom caring for Miss Piggy, there was a mishap and Jack got his last guinea pig. Jonny's mom didn't tell him about it though. Two months later Jonny asked his mom, "Where's Miss Piggy?"

Jonny's mom liked to prepare a healthy tonic for her family. Her tonics didn't taste good, in Jonny's opinion. One day when his mom was preparing a new batch, Jonny and his friend decided to add an ingredient that would make it taste even worse. Since Jonny's mom had promised to taste the tonic before giving it to anyone else, she might decide to throw out the batch.

So Jonny and his friend added crushed earthworm juice when his mom wasn't looking, promising each other not to tell. When Jonny's mom returned to the kitchen, she told Jonny that this would be a good time to sample the new tonic. She even asked his friend if he would like a taste, but he declined.

Jonny reminded her that she should be the first to sample it so she took a tablespoonful. She grimaced but then poured a tablespoon for Jonny. With both his mom and his friend insisting that he drink it, he had no other choice. He had planned to hold it in his mouth and go to the bathroom to spit it out, but his friend held him back, asking how it tasted. Jonny had to swallow it before answering, "Awful!"

Jonny promised to get a chocolate bar and share it with his friend. When he opened the cupboard where his mom kept chocolates and chips and suchlike things, he found a note saying "Get permission before taking anything." Jonny kept his promise.

Jonny and his friend, as an activity toward earning the Green Star at the cub camp, decided to track. Jonny would leave a trail and his friend would follow it. Jonny left a crust of bread at the start, a few crumbs along the way, and the remainder of the slice of bread at the back wall of the tuck shop. His friend followed the trail right to the tuck shop despite the setback of birds having eaten some of the breadcrumbs.

Jonny had helped his friend by giving him a hint where the end of the trail would be. The Cub Scout Promise is "I promise that I will do my best to do my duty to God and to the Queen, to *help other people* and to keep the Cub Scout Law" (emphasis added).

Jonny wrote a poem as a creative activity toward earning the Tawny Star.

> Give some thought to any promise
> You might decide to make
> Make it a bit ambiguous
> But not patently a fake

Jonny thought up his own personal active living program toward earning the Red Star. When playing chess, if capturing an opponent's pawn, the captor would sit on his opponent while his opponent made one pushup. If capturing a bishop or knight, the opponent would have to do three pushups; if a rook, five pushups; if a queen, nine pushups; if a king, in other words when a checkmate, fifteen pushups. (Jonny was heavier than his friend.)

Jonny's friend thought up a game. He had the white king on A1 of the chess board. Jonny had the black king on H1. Jonny's friend tapped his cellphone once and moved his king to A2. Jonny tapped his phone twice and moved to H2. (They both had cellphones that included tap counters as well as timers.) The kings were to work their way to row eight, each move requiring double the number of taps of the previous move. Jonny's friend tapped his phone four times and advanced to A3. Jonny tapped his phone eight times and… During the hour that Jonny spent tapping his phone 8192 times, he regretted allowing his friend to have gone first.

Jonny promised his friend that he would play the card game that his friend liked, 52-card-pickup. This was before he knew what the game was. His friend scattered the cards on the floor. Jonny didn't keep his promise.

Jonny promised that he would *not* join his friend in his game of "squares" as his friend called it. His friend brought out a chocolate bar and began breaking off the squares. Before eating the first he sang,

> Eight squares of choc in the bar
> Gulp one down, don't pass around
> Seven squares of choc in the bar

You can guess what he sang before eating the second square. He made sure Jonny kept his promise.

Jonny's math teacher at school promised to give extra marks for homework handed in and done in ink rather than pencil. This was to encourage neatness. Jonny had been doing math in pencil, erasing mistakes and rewriting. He switched to ink, simply overwriting mistakes.

Jonny's English teacher gave her class a poetry writing assignment. They were to indicate what poetic forms their poems incorporated. Jonny wrote a monometric couplet consisting of two trochees. It incorporated allusion, assonance, enjambment, rhyme, and rhythm. Its title was *Fleas*, followed by:

> Adam
> Had 'em

Jonny and his friend teamed up for a biology project, their teacher having promised extra marks for innovativeness. They got two small boxes and some tubing. The tubing went up from one box to a tee where a tube to the right circled back to the same bare box. A tube to the left went to the second box full of soft earth. Their project was to teach an earthworm to turn left.

Jonny promised his mom that he would go to bed before midnight. He kept his promise. However, he got up shortly after midnight and continued playing computer games.

Jonny had promised to wash his hands before setting the table. (That's putting plates, cups, and cutlery on the table.) When his mother reminded him of his promise, he told her that he had washed his hands. (He had washed them the previous day but had picked his nose several times since. This was when Jonny was a preteen, long before the sanitary practices due to the coronavirus.)

Jonathan told his teenage son Jonny not to go to see his friend. (This was decades later during restrictions on visiting because of the coronavirus.) Jonny promised not to see his friend. He went over to his friend's house and, before entering the house, pulled his mask over his eyes.

ENDNOTES ON CHAPTER 5

The story of Joe and Jody is a figment of my imagination.

Other family stories are loosely based on my childhood and fatherhood.

The saying "A little bird told me" may have originated from a verse in Ecclesiastes,
> Curse not the king, no not in thy thought; and curse
> not the rich in thy bedchamber, for a bird of the air
> shall carry the voice, and that which hath wings
> shall tell the matter (Eccles. 10:20).

Jesus' parable of the Good Samaritan can be found in Luke 10, verses 30 to 35.

The parable of the wicked servant can be found in Matthew 18, verses 23 to 34. When quoting verse 23, I omitted the word "therefore" and changed the word order slightly.

In the story of Jonny, Jack and Miss Piggy, names have been changed to protect identities.

In the last story, Jonny could also be called Junior.

CHAPTER 6

PROMISES, PLEDGES, VOWS, AND OATHS

Definitions

A *promise* is a declaration that one will do something or that a particular thing will happen. A couple of Hebrew words translated as *promise* merely mean something said. A Greek word often translated as *promise* could also be translated as *announcement*.

A *pledge* is a security payment or down payment, or something given guaranteeing the payment of a debt. A Greek word for *pledge*, derived from a Hebrew word, could also mean *deposit*.

A *vow* is a solemn promise or a voluntary offering. The Greek word translated as *vow* can mean, on occasion, a prayer to God.

An *oath* is a solemn promise before God or, in the negative sense, a curse. A Greek word translated *oath* can mean that which has been pledged or promised with an oath.

Promises

> That which is gone out of thy lips thou shalt keep
> and perform, even a freewill offering, according as
> thou hast vowed unto the LORD thy God, which
> thou hast promised with thy mouth.

Two different Hebrew words are used, translated as *vowed* and *promised*. In this case promising to give a freewill offering is equated with vowing to make the offering. In the time of Moses, commitments were made orally. Nowadays, in court, an oral agreement is not considered as binding as a written agreement.

A promised offering to the Lord in Moses' day could be similar these days to an offering made to a church or religious organization. As with freewill offerings, those officiating over the congregation benefit from the offering. These days, we need the Holy Spirit's help when deciding who we are going to benefit.

Sometimes a pledge is arranged so that a certain amount is automatically withdrawn from a person's bank account. If a person felt too generous when making the pledge, he might later realize he can't afford it. Cancelling a pledge may not seem as serious as breaking a vow, but there are similarities.

Another rash promise is pledging security for a friend or acquaintance. A proverb begins,

> My son, if thou be surety for thy friend, if thou hast
> stricken thy hand with a stranger, thou art snared
> with the words of thy mouth, thou art taken with
> the words of thy mouth.

The proverb continues with the advice to plead to be extricated from the pledge.

> Do this now, my son, and deliver thyself, when thou
> art come into the hand of thy friend; go, humble
> thyself, and make sure thy friend.

The clause "and make sure thy friend" might otherwise be translated "and press your plea with your friend." It's humbling to beg for mercy.

When I was a youth, the father of a friend told me he had lost his home by pledging that he would pay in case another person defaulted on his debt. He advised me never to pledge security for anyone.

I have, however, put in a good word for someone I suspected might not be so reliable. She had put my name and phone number down as a reference. I tried to talk about her good qualities without mentioning the bad ones.

In this case, I was helping a person who had trusted me for a good report while perhaps doing a disservice for her potential employer. Withholding relevant information is a tactic sometimes used by lawyers.

Considering pleading to be extricated from a pledge, it could also apply to pleading with the Lord. If we have made a bad pledge or vow to the Lord, we should humble ourselves and plead for forgiveness. Of course, if the pledge involved people, we need to approach them as well. For example, if we pledged to tithe to a particular church but then unexpected expenses came up, we might ask to be excused from paying the tithe. On the other hand, the situation might be the Lord's test to see if we will continue to tithe and trust the Lord for additional income.

Third Best

About a millennium after Moses' directives on freewill offerings, the prophet Malachi pronounced a curse on anyone failing to fulfil his vow. "But cursed be the deceiver, which hath in his flock a male, and voweth, and sacrificeth unto the Lord a corrupt thing." This does not necessarily suggest that a female is a corrupt thing.

The sin that Malachi addressed was vowing to give God the best but then giving him something defective. A defective animal was acceptable as a freewill offering, but not as a vow. Malachi implied that it would be better not to sacrifice anything at all.

The Lord does deserve the best, but ranchers like to save the best for breeding. Only the Lord, however, knows which animals are really the best for breeding. A first-rate yearling usually has good genes, but another may have equally good genes. Then it depends which sperm out of millions fertilizes the egg. God controls chance.

A Way Out

For those who realized they made a rash vow, there was a way out–confession and compensation.

> Whatsoever it be that a man shall pronounce with an oath, and it be hid from him; when he knoweth of it…he shall confess that he hath sinned in that thing. And he shall bring his trespass offering unto the LORD for his sin which he hath sinned.

In summery and in modern English this would read, "If anyone utters a rash oath, when he realizes its foolishness, he must admit his guilt and make compensation for the sin he has committed."

A person can sin unknowingly. In this case the sin may have resulted from the human tendency to judge when not knowing enough about the situation.

Imagining a possible rash promise during the time of Moses, perhaps it had been arranged for a young man to marry a particular young lady. However, the young man heard a derogatory rumour about her. He vowed that he wouldn't marry her. Later he heard that the rumour was wrong. (It may have been started by another young lady who was jealous.)

When he realized the vow he had made was wrong, he needed to confess his sin and, before marrying the young lady, bring his trespass offering to the Lord.

Moses wrote guidelines for priests when dealing with a man wanting to extricate himself from a vow or pledge that he had made. He might have offered himself or a member of his family in service to the priests of the sanctuary.

He could be freed from this service by making a payment. The priest was to estimate how much the person making the pledge should pay in order to be released from it.

> And thy estimation shall be of the male from twenty years old even unto sixty years old…fifty shekels.
>
> And if it be a female…thirty shekels.
>
> And if it be from five years old even unto twenty years old, then thy estimation shall be of the male twenty shekels, and for the female ten shekels.
>
> And if it be from a month old even unto five years old, then thy estimation shall be of the male five shekels of silver, and for the female…three shekels.
>
> And if it be from sixty years old and above, if it be a male then thy estimation shall be fifteen shekels, and for the female ten shekels.
>
> But if he be poorer than thy estimation, then he shall present himself before the priest, and the priest shall value him.

Those between twenty and sixty years of age were valued highest because they would be capable of the greatest service. Youth between five and twenty were valued less, and children under five were valued less yet. Those over sixty were valued below youth but above children.

The poor were rated according to their ability to pay. No one was freed from at least some payment.

If this can be taken as an evaluation of a person's worth, I see that I am valued between a child and a youth. The amount of my pension does suggest this.

MALES AND FEMALES

The law about paying to be released from a pledge also valued the service of males higher than that of females. Females were considered to be between a half and two-thirds as useful as males. Service in the sanctuary, therefore, must have been different from work in the family tent. Generally speaking, women and girls in those days would have been more proficient than men and boys at cooking, sewing, and cleaning.

If females being rated at about three-fifths the value of males is an indication of inequality, then females must have evolved over the millennia to what they are now–equal to men. On the other hand, some believe humans are devolving rather than evolving. In that case, men must have degenerated at a faster rate than women.

Another law differentiated between a man making a vow and a woman making a vow. A man should never break his word.

> This is the thing which the LORD hath commanded. If a man vow a vow unto the LORD, or swear an oath to bind his soul with a bond, he shall not break his word, he shall do according to all that proceedeth out of his mouth.

The vow of a young woman could be broken by her father.

> If a woman also vow a vow unto the LORD, and bind herself by a bond, being in her father's house in her youth; and her father hear her vow, and her bond

wherewith she hath bound her soul, and her father
disallow her in the day that he heareth, not any of
her vows, or of her bonds wherewith she hath bound
her soul, shall stand, and the LORD shall forgive
her, because her father disallowed her.

The vow of a wife could be broken by her husband.

And if she had at all an husband, when she vowed, or
uttered ought out of her lips, wherewith she bound
her soul, and her husband heard it, and disallowed
her on the day that he heard it, then he shall make
her vow which she vowed, and that which she uttered
with her lips, wherewith she bound her soul, of none
effect, and the LORD shall forgive her.

Another translation, instead of "uttered ought out of her lips,"
reads "made some rash promise." Instead of "that which she uttered
with her lips," it is translated "the rash promise of her lips."

I wonder if these laws still apply. If a father hears his daughter
vowing to become a nun, he would have to annul her vow as soon
as he heard it. Then she could renew her vow out of his hearing. If a
husband hears his wife pledging to give money to charity, he could
object if he were the income earner of the family.

Better Not

A millennium and a half after Moses, the apostle Paul advised that
young widows shouldn't be supported by the church, for when their
passions overcame their dedication to Christ, they would remarry.
Thus they would bring judgment on themselves because they would
have broken their previous commitment. Although none of the
Greek words are used for promise, pledge, vow, or oath, this is an
interpretation of what the apostle Paul meant.

These days, few young widows are supported by the church. Some widows get a survivor's pension or social security benefits for themselves or their children. If the support would be reduced if they got married, it might be financially better for them to live in a common-law relationship. A common-law relationship, some say, is like marriage without the vows.

On the subject of oaths, Jesus said about backing up one's word with an oath, "Swear not at all. But let your communication be 'Yea, yea; nay, nay' for whatsoever is more than these cometh of evil."

It seems that Jesus was countering the hypocrisy of the religious leaders of his time. They were saying that it made a difference whether an oath was made in public or in private and whether the name of God was used to back up the oath or merely reference made to heaven, earth, or Jerusalem. A private oath emphasized with "by heaven" was not binding, according to the religious leaders.

We should simply say "yes" or "no." (I sometimes say "maybe.") If asked whether we are going to do something or go somewhere, a better answer than "yes" or "no" might be "I plan to" or "I don't plan to." This allows for a change of plans. True, we should try to keep commitments.

An example of an acceptable breaking of a commitment would be if I got invited to talk about my book on a radio show but I had previously promised to go to a birthday party at the same time. An example of an unacceptable breaking of a commitment would be if the birthday party that I had promised to go to were for the publisher of my book. These days, what is acceptable and what is unacceptable is a subjective opinion.

Jesus' brother, James, said more or less the same thing as Jesus about not emphasizing with oaths. "Swear not, neither by heaven, neither by the earth, neither by any other oath, but let your yea be yea, and your nay, nay, lest ye fall into condemnation."

An exception to the command "Swear not" might be when required to swear in court to tell the truth, the whole truth, and nothing but the truth. With marriage vows, although God or heaven or earth or Jerusalem may not be mentioned, the vows need to be taken seriously.

According to James, simply saying we will do something could be rash. He reprimands men who say they will go on a business trip today or tomorrow.

> Whereas ye know not what shall be on the morrow. For what is your life? It is even a vapour, that appeareth for a little time, and then vanisheth away. For that ye ought to say, If the Lord will, we shall live, and do this, or that.

David's Vow

It is a rash promise if someone promises to do something but then doesn't do it because of a change of circumstance. A scriptural example of this is when David was in the wilderness avoiding King Saul. He had sent some of his young men to ask a favour of a wealthy landowner named Nabal.

Nabal, however, responded with insults. Then David, strapping on his sword, set out with four hundred of his men to take vengeance on Nabal. He vowed, "So and more also do God unto the enemies of David, if I leave of all that pertain to him by the morning light any that pisseth against the wall."

David was invoking a curse if he left alive any male of all who belonged to Nabal. Allowing for readers' sensitivities, most modern translations paraphrase David's vow as pertaining to males. David planned to kill the men and older boys of Nabal's household. Women, girls, and boys too young to walk wouldn't be pissing against the wall.

The wall would probably have been one dedicated to such a purpose. It may have had a little trench at the base to contain the piss so that pissers wouldn't get their feet wet.

Nabal's wife Abigail, however, hearing that David was coming, met him to apologize for Nabal's behaviour. She presented David and his men with an ample supply of food.

David changed his mind about killing Nabal and the menfolk of his family. He praised the Lord for inspiring Abigail to meet him and keep him from murder.

ENDNOTES ON CHAPTER 6

The definitions of *promise, pledge, vow,* and *oath* are my summaries of the definitions of Hebrew and Greek words that are translated into the English words. I looked them up in Strong's Exhaustive Concordance.

The verse where Moses used two different words translated as *vowed* and *promised* is Deuteronomy 23, verse 23.

The proverb about not pledging security is in Proverbs 6, verses 1 to 5. The quote is verses 1 to 3.

The prophet Malachi pronounced God's curse on a man who promises to give God his best but then gives him less than his best. The quote is part of Malachi 1, verse 14.

With freewill offerings, a defective animal could be offered. See Leviticus 22, verse 23.

If someone makes a rash vow, when he realizes its foolishness, he must admit his guilt and make compensation. I quoted parts of Leviticus 5, verses 4 to 6.

Moses' law guiding priests when dealing with a man making a vow or pledge is in Leviticus 27. I quoted parts of verses 1 to 7.

Another law differentiated between a man making a vow or oath or pledge and a woman doing the same. The quote is from Numbers 30, verses 2 to 8. *Bond* is the word the King James translators used instead of *pledge* and *to bind his soul* instead of to *obligate himself.*

The apostle Paul's instruction concerning young widows is from 1 Timothy 5, verses 11 and 12. "But the younger widows refuse, for when they have begun to wax wanton against Christ, they will marry, having damnation, because they have cast off their first faith."

Jesus' directive about not swearing can be found in Matthew 5, verses 34 to 37. The quote is part of verse 34 and all of verse 37. Swearing, in this case, is invoking divine recognition, not blasphemy as in taking the Lord's name in vain.

Jesus' brother, James, advised people to say simply "yes" or "no" and not to try to back it up with an oath. The quote is part of James 5, verse 12.

James also reprimanded the overly self-confident. The quote is James 4, verses 14 to 15.

The account of David and Nabal and Abigail can be found in 1 Samuel 25. David's promise is in verse 22.

CHAPTER 7

To Blaspheme, Curse, Swear, Profane

Definitions

To blaspheme is to speak irreverently about God or sacred things, to condemn, despise, abhor, or revile. A Hebrew word which usually means to bless is sometimes translated to blaspheme. The Greek word translated as *blaspheme* can also mean to speak reproachfully, rail at or defame.

To curse is to utter offensive words in annoyance or to treat with contempt. It can also mean to put a curse on, or be under a curse. A Greek word meaning to bind under a curse can apply to oneself, to declare oneself liable to the severest divine penalties.

To swear is to use offensive language, especially as an expression of anger (the negative meaning only). The Greek word translated as *to swear* means, in the positive sense, to affirm or to promise, but in the negative sense, to threaten with an oath.

To profane is to treat something sacred with irreverence or disrespect, to pollute or cause to be defiled. In both Hebrew and Greek, it can imply simply making something secular or public, accessible to everyone.

BLASPHEMY

Jews and Christians are familiar with the command, "Thou shalt not take the name of the LORD thy God in vain." Blasphemy would be disobeying this command.

But what is God's name? Hebrew scribes wrote only the consonants of the name so we are not sure how it was pronounced. It may have sounded something like "Yahweh," otherwise translated as "Jehovah." The name "Jehovah" has too many syllables to be an effective swear word.

Moses decreed execution for someone who blasphemed. "And he that blasphemeth the name of the LORD, he shall surely be put to death, and all the congregation shall certainly stone him."

Moses' verdict concerned an Egyptite who had cursed. (*Egyptite* is a name I made up for a child of an Egyptian and an Israelite.) He had been in a fight and it seemed that his temper flared. People sometimes say rash things when they are angry.

Moses sought the Lord's direction on what the Egyptite's punishment should be. It turned out to be execution. Those who had heard him curse were to lay their hands on his head and then all the congregation should stone him.

I imagine women, girls, and boys would be excluded from those stoning him. Their aim might not have been so good, hitting instead the guys with their hands on the Egyptite's head.

The severe punishment for the Egyptite was not discrimination against someone of mixed blood. The law applied to all the Hebrews at that time. But God may not approve of such a drastic punishment these days.

Causing a Curse

We tend to think of blaspheming, cursing and swearing as being similar, but there are distinctions. Cursing can mean putting a curse on someone, for example, pronouncing a curse upon a liar. Amongst Moses' "shall nots" is the command, "Ye shall not swear by my name falsely."

If a husband suspected his wife of being unfaithful, he could take her to the priest.

> And the priest shall bring her near, and set her before the LORD; and the priest shall take holy water in an earthen vessel, and of the dust that is in the floor of the tabernacle the priest shall take, and put it into the water;
>
> And the priest shall charge her by an oath, and say unto the woman, "If no man have lain with thee, and if thou hast not gone aside to uncleanness with another instead of thy husband, be thou free from this bitter water that causeth the curse; but if thou hast gone aside to another instead of thy husband, and if thou be defiled, and some man have lain with thee beside thine husband,"
>
> Then the priest shall charge the woman with an oath of cursing, and the priest shall say unto the woman, "The LORD make thee a curse and an oath among thy people, when the LORD doth make thy thigh to rot, and thy belly to swell; and this water that causeth the curse shall go into thy bowels, to make thy belly to swell, and thy thigh to rot." And the woman shall say, "Amen, amen."
>
> And the priest shall write these curses in a book, and he shall blot them out with the bitter water; and he shall cause the woman to drink the bitter water that causeth the curse, and the water that causeth the curse shall enter into her, and become bitter.

The holy water was probably water from the laver where the priests washed their hands and feet. I trust that the dust from the dirt floor of the tabernacle would not have had many mouse droppings in it.

Blotting out the curses with the bitter water probably meant washing the ink on the parchment into the bitter water. The ink may have been made from carbon black collected from something burnt. (I'm reminded of a fuel sometimes used in the Middle East–dried cow patties.)

Parchment in those days was made from specially prepared, untanned skins of sheep or goats. The woman being tested should have been thankful that the skin was untanned as tanning in those days was done with urine.

The outcome of the test seemed to be that if the woman were guilty, her abdomen would swell and her womb shrink, as one translation interprets it. God can cause curses to come true.

The Hebrew verb translated *go aside*, as when the priest asked the woman if she had gone aside to a man other than her husband, can apply to men also. A proverb warns young men not to go aside or "decline" to the ways of a strange woman. "Let not thine heart decline to her [the strange woman's] ways."

A dictionary definition of strange is "difficult to understand or explain." That may define all women.

COUNTER-CURSE

In the case of the woman and the priests, *believing* in the power of a curse gave it power. In the sophisticated West, we generally don't attach much weight to curses, but there *are* spiritual powers that influence our lives.

I don't have a personal example, but when travelling in Africa I heard several accounts of witch doctors cursing people so that they got sick or died. Here is a more recent account of a threatened curse and counter-curse. Part of the letter reads,

Pastor Henry was approached by the leader of the witches and shamans in Coopertown to tell him they don't want him there and he must close down or be cursed. After calling Pastor Eric, and they had prayer, Pastor Eric addressed this leader telling him to stay away from Pastor Henry and his church or he would be dead in two days. This declaration was ignored and further harassment ensued but in two days the witch doctor became very ill and did die. The witchdoctor's replacement also returned to the church to harass Pastor Henry and again Pastor Eric was there to show Pastor Henry how to deal with this demonic oppression, and the replacement witch also died. Pastor Henry was now equipped to deal with this but so far no one has returned as they are all afraid.

SWEARING

In my previous workplaces, and in other situations also, I have heard many swear words. In one work place where they knew I was a Christian, someone even apologized for swearing in front of me. Rather than remaining quiet, it may have been better for me to have said something. A conversation might have gone like this:

Me: Did I just hear you refer to a barrier that holds back water?
Him: Ha ha! But this blanketly blank thing...
Me: Well, swearing won't help. Who knows? God may be listening.
Him: Think so?
Me: Jesus said that if you are even angry with someone, you are subject to judgement, and if you curse someone, you are in danger of hellfire.
Him: I'd better watch what I say then!

I myself didn't swear much before I came to know the Lord. But the little that I did, and being accustomed to hearing others swearing, made me uncomfortable saying "Jesus" in a positive sense.

Profanity

We think of profanity as blasphemous or obscene language, but the Hebrew and Greek words translated as *profanity* also have the meaning of irreverence. The quote about not swearing falsely "Ye shall not swear by my name falsely" continues with "neither shalt thou profane the name of thy God." To profane God's name means to dishonour God.

The apostle Paul wrote, "Shun profane and vain babblings: for they will increase unto more ungodliness." Christians should avoid irreverent and worthless talk. It's not a good witness. And being accustomed to a little ungodliness can lead people into more and more ungodliness. Like cancer, it spreads.

We shouldn't revile others either. The apostle Peter wrote about arrogant people who despise government, scoffing at things they do not understand. "Presumptuous are they, selfwilled, they are not afraid to speak evil of dignities."

He wrote that letter shortly before his martyrdom under the corrupt rule of the Roman Emperor Nero. Although some dignitaries actually were evil, it was rash to speak evil about them; an evil speaker could get executed. Roman citizens were often beheaded while others might have been crucified.

Christians were persecuted not so much because they spoke out against the evil emperor but because they were proclaiming Jesus to be the righteous ruler over all. In our time, living in what is described as a democracy, we should be cautious when criticizing our leaders. Moses instructed, "Thou shalt not... curse the ruler of thy people."

IN INDIA

In India, cows are sacred to the Hindus. They believe cows represent divine and natural beneficence. I remember watching a fruit vendor to see what he would do as a cow approached his stall. He was not supposed to deny food to a cow. The cow stopped, then turned away. I assume the vendor gave the cow a don't-you-dare look.

In my youth, I occasionally expressed wonder by using an expression suggesting the holiness attributed to cows. But by attributing holiness to something profane, we dishonour God. Hindus may object to my suggestion that cows are profane. But the cows I saw in India didn't seem any holier than the cows on the farm in Canada, and those cows didn't have any aspect of holiness about them.

The holy book of the Hindu's, the Bhagavad Gita, may or may not include a law similar to one of Moses' laws, that profane people should be stoned to death. If I had been driving in India and if I had accidentally hit a cow, I might have gotten stoned. (Actually, I did get "stoned" in India.)

IMPIETY

An expression of disgust is "Good Lord!" It is true that the Lord is good and can turn even bad situations into good ones *for those who love God.* "All things work together for good to them that love God." But people irreverently saying "Good Lord!" may have things working out for their *harm.* To balance blessings there are curses, and there may not be much in between. The Lord notes everything we say.

Words that are associated with God might be used in an irreverent way. In the Bible school that I attended, there were many p.k.s and m.k.s (pastors' kids and missionaries' kids). They knew Scripture well, but my esteem for them plummeted when I heard one of them burp and then say "amen."

BAD EXAMPLE

In chapter 4, I wrote about King Antiochus during the time of the Maccabees. I'll continue.

King Antiochus got killed in battle and Demetrius became the new king. King Demetrius, like King Antiochus, disliked the rebel Maccabees. He chose a man by the name of Bacchides "and commanded that he should take vengeance of the children of Israel. They [Bacchides and those with him] sent messengers to Judas [Judas Maccabeus] and his brethren with peaceable words deceitfully. But they gave no heed to their words."

Some priests and religious Jews, however, did agree to meet with Bacchides, "so he spake unto them peaceably, and sware unto them, saying, we will procure the harm neither of you nor your friends. Whereupon they believed him: howbeit he took of them threescore men, and slew them in one day." Bacchides, like King Antiochus, didn't keep his word.

King Demetrius later sent another agent, Nicanor, to Jerusalem. When the priests refused to hand over Judas Maccabeus to him, Nicanor mocked them, "and sware in his wrath, saying, 'Unless Judas and his host be now delivered into my hands, if ever I come again in safety, I will burn up this house' [the temple]."

Both the priests and Judas prayed that the Lord would judge Nicanor for his blasphemy. Judas assembled his fighting men and faced Nicanor and his troops in battle. Judas won and Nicanor was killed. His head and his right arm that he had held out toward the temple when he made the oath were cut off and taken to Jerusalem. So Nicanor's rash promise cost him an arm and a head (rather than an arm and a leg).

Endnotes on Chapter 7

The definitions of *to blaspheme, curse, swear,* and *profane* are my summaries of the definitions of Hebrew and Greek words that are translated into the English words. I looked them up in Strong's Exhaustive Concordance.

The quote from the Ten Commandments is part of Exodus 20, verse 7 (repeated in Deut. 5:11). The complete verse is "Thou shalt not take the name of the LORD thy God in vain, for the LORD will not hold him guiltless that taketh his name in vain."

The story of a man who blasphemed being stoned to death is in Leviticus 24. In verse 11 it is said that he blasphemed the name of the Lord and cursed. Verse 14 refers to him who cursed. The quoted verdict that he be stoned to death is part of verse 16.

The quote about swearing falsely is part of Leviticus 19, verse 12. The complete verse is "And ye shall not swear by my name falsely, neither shalt thou profane the name of thy God: I am the LORD."

The test for an unfaithful wife is in Numbers 5. The quote is verses 16 and 17 and verses 19 to 24.

Men also are warned not to succumb to the allure of a strange woman. "Let not thine heart decline to her ways, go not astray in her paths" (Prov. 7:25). The quote is part of this verse.

For further information about pastor Eric in Africa, contact Helen Fletcher at helen@visionimpactliberia.org.

Jesus said, "But I tell you that anyone who is angry with a brother or sister will be subject to judgment. Again, anyone who says to a brother or sister, 'Raca,' is answerable to the court. And anyone who says, 'You fool!' will be in danger of the fire of hell" (Matt. 5:22).

The apostle Paul wrote, "But shun profane and vain babblings: for they will increase unto more ungodliness" (2 Tim. 2:16).

The apostle Peter wrote about those who despise authority, "Presumptuous are they, selfwilled, they are not afraid to speak evil of dignities" (part of 2 Pet. 2:10). The following verse condemns their rash accusations, saying that even angels do not dare to bring a charge of blasphemy against them.

Moses instructed, "Thou shalt not revile the gods, nor curse the ruler of thy people" (Ex. 22:28). I quoted part of this verse.

The apostle Paul wrote, "And we know that all things work together for good to them that love God, to them who are the called according to his purpose" (Rom. 8:28). The quote is part of this verse.

The quotes of King Demetrius, Bacchides, and Nicanor trying to subjugate the Jews are taken from 1 Maccabees 7. Chapters 14 and 15 of 2 Maccabees give a more detailed account of Nicanor's dealings with the Jews and of his death. 2 Maccabees 14, verse 33 says that it was Nicanor's right hand that he had stretched out toward the temple. 2 Maccabees 15, verse 30 says that his arm was cut off at the shoulder.

CHAPTER 8

THE STORY OF JACOB

"For the Lord has chosen Jacob unto himself."

Although Jacob became his mother's favourite, he did cause her extra difficulty at birth. When grasping his twin brother's heel as they passed through the birth canal, his arm beside his head must have made giving birth a yet more painful ordeal.

Perhaps, in the womb, he had overheard the Lord's promise to his mother, Rebekah, that the older would serve the younger. By hanging onto Esau's heel, he made Esau help him emerge to the outside world.

Thinking of the Lord's promise to Rebekah, the Lord may not have introduced himself by name when making that promise. She recognized, however, that it was the God of Isaac and Abraham that made the promise.

Buying the Birthright

As the boys grew up, Esau became a skillful hunter but Jacob was a homebody. One day when Jacob was cooking some stew, Esau arrived home from the countryside exhausted and hungry.

Esau said to Jacob, "Feed me, I pray thee, with that same red pottage."

Jacob replied, "Sell me this day thy birthright." The birthright in this case meant inheriting, upon their father's death, a double portion of what other brothers would inherit.

Esau said, "Behold, I am at the point to die, and what profit shall this birthright do to me?"

And Jacob said, "Swear to me this day."

Then Esau swore that Jacob could have his birthright. Thus, Esau despised his birthright.

Rash promises are often made in the heat of the moment. We don't know what emotion Esau might have had, but perhaps he was disappointed because of not managing to shoot any game that day. Perhaps he looked down on his brother who had stayed home doing "women's work." Perhaps Jacob teased him, tasting the stew and saying "Yum yum."

Esau has gone down in history as a profane person "who for one morsel of meat sold his birthright." That doesn't mean that Jacob had added a little meat to the stew. In modern-day English "one morsel of meat" means "a single meal."

I remember my Grade 2 teacher reading the story of Jacob and Esau to us students. (These days, public school teachers wouldn't be allowed to read Bible stories to students.) She read from the King James Version, which describes lentil stew as red pottage. I confused pottage with porridge and wondered what would make porridge red. Red currants might.

Obtaining the Blessing

Jacob's mother persuaded Jacob to trick his blind father into giving him the blessing meant for the eldest son. At first Jacob was reluctant, saying that perhaps his father would realize that it was a trick and would curse him instead of blessing him.

Rebekah responded, "Upon me be thy curse, my son; only obey my voice."

So Jacob obeyed his mother and tricked his father into blessing him instead of Esau. Isaac's blessing ended with a pronouncement,

> Let people serve thee, and nations bow down to thee:
> be lord over thy brethren, and let thy mother's sons
> bow down to thee: cursed be every one that curseth
> thee, and blessed be he that blesseth thee.

Isaac realized later that he had been tricked, but wouldn't take back his blessing on Jacob. And God did bless Jacob even with Jacob's continued tendency to be conniving.

Esau complained to his father about his brother,

> Is not he rightly named Jacob? for he hath supplanted
> me these two times; he took away my birthright and,
> behold, now he hath taken away my blessing. (The
> name "Jacob" has the connotation of "deceiver.")

Although Esau regretted selling his birthright and losing the blessing reserved for the eldest son, "he found no place of repentance, though he sought it carefully with tears." Instead of being repentant he was resentful.

Jacob may or may not have actually inherited a double portion of his father's estate. A few centuries later, however, Jacob's descendants did take over the land where Isaac once lived.

The other portion of the inheritance for the firstborn was judicial and spiritual authority. Jacob did receive that authority as is suggested by his name change. That change occurred years later when he was returning to the land where his father Isaac lived. A man, probably an angel, when wrestling with Jacob, told him, "Thy name shall be called no more Jacob, but Israel." Israel means "he strives with God."

Nowadays the name "Israel" causes us to think of a land where the descendants of Jacob have authority over any descendants of Esau or Ishmael living in the land. In fact, few people these days consider themselves to be descendants of Esau. His descendants, the Edomites, eventually assimilated with surrounding nations.

"Cursed be every one that curseth thee, and blessed be he that blesseth thee," Isaac had pronounced over Jacob. Although many people don't make the connection, there does seem to be a curse on those who curse Israel and a blessing on those who bless Israel.

TRAVELLING TO HARAN

When Jacob was fleeing from his revengeful brother, he stopped for the night, sleeping out in the open. For a pillow he took a stone. People in those days apparently used much harder pillows than we like to use these days. Perhaps Jacob indulged a bit, putting a skin over the stone.

During the night Jacob dreamt of a ladder stretching from earth to heaven, with angels ascending and descending on it. Standing above the ladder, the Lord promised to give Jacob and his descendants the land on which Jacob was lying. We assume the Lord meant more than just the small plot of earth on which Jacob was lying.

When Jacob woke up, he turned his pillow into a pillar to commemorate the Lord's promise. Then he poured oil on it. Speculating on what that oil might have been, it may have been olive oil that he had brought with him in which to dip his bread. He may have been carrying the oil in a skin because a clay pot would have been heavy to lug all the way from Beersheba to Haran.

Jacob named the place Bethel, which means House of God, and made a conditional vow that if the Lord would be with him and provide for him so that he returned to his father's house in peace, then the Lord would be his God. He would give back to the Lord a tenth of all that the Lord gave him.

Why did Jacob choose to give the Lord a tenth and not an eighth or a twelfth? The regional number system seems to have been based on ten, so then he would merely have had to move the decimal point one digit to the left to arrive at the promised tenth. (But isn't Hebrew written from right to left?)

A precedent for giving a tenth was Jacob's grandfather Abraham giving a tenth to Melchizedek, king of Salem. Melchizedek was said to be priest of God Most High.

We learn, as the story of Jacob continues, that God did bless him abundantly. Upon Jacob's return to Bethel, he apparently did sacrifice some of his flock.

Earning Some Wives

When Jacob arrived in Haran and met up with his relatives, he was warmly welcomed. However, his uncle Laban made some rather deceptive promises. He promised that Jacob could marry his daughter Rachel if Jacob would work for him for seven years. That would be instead of Jacob paying a dowry.

For the wedding, however, Laban substituted his older daughter Leah. Bridal veils in those days must not have been the see-through kind. Actually, it could well have been Rachel during the wedding feast, but that night when it was dark, Laban took Leah to Jacob.

When Jacob woke up in the morning, he discovered that he had slept with Leah! He confronted Laban about the deception and Laban said that he could also marry Rachel if he agreed to work for him another seven years.

Laban changed Jacob's wages while Jacob was working for him. Jacob complained to his wives, "Your father hath deceived me, and changed my wages ten times."

Later, accusing Laban himself, Jacob said, "Thou hast changed my wages ten times."

Laban's failure to keep his promises to Jacob didn't pay off. He ended up losing his daughters and much of his flock to his son-in-law.

FLEEING FROM LABAN

When Jacob and his household fled from Haran, Laban caught up with them. Laban accused them of stealing his gods. (Laban's father and grandfather, seemingly, were idol makers.) Not knowing that Rachel had taken the idols, Jacob replied, "With whomsoever thou findest thy gods, let him not live."

Laban searched for them, even in Rachel's tent where she had hidden them, but he didn't find them. (That must have been demeaning for the idols, being sat upon by a woman claiming to be menstruating.)

If Laban had found the idols, Rachel probably would not have been executed. Curses, however, register with God. Although the curse depended on Laban finding the idols, Rachel's untimely death later may have been God's punishment. It seems Rachel had a tendency toward idolatry, which is not at all a good thing.

Jacob and Laban swore by the God of their forefathers not to harm each other. "Jacob sware by the fear of his father Isaac." They kept their promise, though the descendants of Jacob and the descendants of Laban were often at war with each other.

Journeying to Bethel

On the way to Bethel, Jacob camped within sight of the town of Shechem. His daughter, Dinah, went to visit the women there and the son of the ruler of the area seduced her. When he and his father came to ask for her hand in marriage, Dinah's brothers made a deceptive promise. He could marry her only if he and all the men of Shechem were circumcised.

The son and father agreed to the terms and persuaded all the men of Shechem also to be circumcised. (The Hivites may have had bronze knives. Circumcising with flint stones would have been yet more painful.)

Three days later, while all of them were still in pain, two of Dinah's brothers took their swords and attacked the unsuspecting town, killing every male. Then the other sons of Jacob came and looted the town.

Jacob journeyed on to Bethel (House of God) and built an altar there. Jacob had promised to give back to God a tenth of all that God would give him. That may have meant sacrificing a tenth of his livestock, and he had accumulated a lot of livestock.

Perhaps Jacob merely roasted the meat rather than burning it all up, but eating a tenth of the flock, even over several weeks, would have meant stuffing themselves. And it wouldn't have been that much of a sacrifice.

Tithing

Thinking of what it would have meant for Jacob to tithe, it would not be too difficult to calculate if it were only a one-time offering. And, if he continued to be scheming, he could select animals that had seen their best years. Would the offering need to be made all at once, however?

If Jacob were to continue tithing the following year, he might calculate a tenth of the *increase* of his flocks and herds. As lambs, kids, and calves are usually born in spring, this could mean calculating the tenth at that time of year (sort of like the tax season).

Would he slaughter them when the meat was nice and tender, say when they were a month old, or would he wait till a year after they were born? And what about donkeys and camels? Instead of slaughtering them, edible animals should be substituted for them.

How should we calculate what portion of our produce to tithe? If we sell fruit from our fruit trees, we can calculate a tenth of the revenue. But if we report the sale and later pay taxes on it, that complicates the situation. Tithing may need to be before taxes, deducting an estimate of the expenses incurred when growing the fruit.

But what if we ourselves eat the fruit from our trees and the vegetables from our garden? Do we have to calculate the value of what we have eaten and tithe on that? Simplest would be just to give away a tenth of the fruit and vegetables. More than a tenth of the zucchinis might be substituted for strawberries if the strawberry crop was poor.

To whom should we give a tenth of our produce? We could give some to our neighbours who have different fruit trees and vegetables from those we have. Then they might give us some of their produce. Especially favourable would be a neighbour with chickens and eggs.

Conniving doesn't work with God, however. It did seem to work out in Jacob's favour only because he was seeking the Lord's favour. He was not conniving in the same manner as his uncle Laban was conniving, nor acting rashly like his brother Esau.

Much later before he died in Egypt, Jacob made his son Joseph swear in a manner he would never forget. He told Joseph, "Put, I pray thee, thy hand under my thigh, and deal kindly and truly with me; bury me not, I pray thee, in Egypt."

Joseph kept that promise.

Endnotes on Chapter 8

"For the LORD hath chosen Jacob unto himself, and Israel for his peculiar treasure" (Ps. 135:4, the complete verse).

The account of the birth of Jacob and Esau is in Genesis 25, verses 24 to 26. The Lord's promise to their mother, Rebekah, is in verse 23.

Genesis 25, verses 29 to 34, records Esau selling his birthright. Esau complained that Jacob took both his birthright and his blessing from him. (Gen. 27:36)

The writer of the Book of Hebrews warns people to be careful "lest there be any fornicator, or profane person, as Esau, who for one morsel of meat sold his birthright. For ye know how that afterward, when he would have inherited the blessing, he was rejected, for he found no place of repentance, though he sought it carefully with tears" (Heb. 12:16–17).

The account of Rebekah pronouncing a curse upon herself is in Genesis 27. The quote is part of verse 13.

Isaac's blessing of his son Jacob is in Genesis 27, verses 28 and 29. The quote is verse 29.

Jacob was renamed Israel. An angel had been wrestling with Jacob, "And he said, 'Thy name shall be called no more Jacob, but Israel: for as a prince hast thou power with God and with men, and hast prevailed'" (Gen. 32:28).

The account of Jacob and the ladder and Jacob's vow to the Lord is in Genesis 28, verses 10 to 22. The ladder may have resembled a staircase more than a ladder.

Abraham gave Melchizedek a tenth of the spoil. See Genesis 14, verses 18 to 20.

The account of Laban substituting his eldest daughter, Leah, for Rachel is in Genesis 29, verse 22.

Jacob's complaint about Laban changing his wages ten times is in Genesis 31, verses 7 and 41.

Jacob's pronouncement of a death sentence for the person who took Laban's idols is in Genesis 31, verse 32.

The account of Jacob and Laban swearing by the God of their forefathers is in Genesis 31, verses 51 to 53. For both of them, Terah was their great-grandfather. Their grandfathers and fathers were Nahor and Bethuel in Laban's case, and Abraham and Isaac in Jacob's case. Jacob swearing by the fear of his father Isaac probably refers to God whom Isaac revered.

The account of Dinah and the Hivites and of Jacob's sons' deceitful promise to Shechem is in Genesis 34, verses 1 to 17.

When he returned to Bethel, Jacob built an altar, probably sacrificing some of his flock on it. See Genesis 35, verses 6 and 7. This was hundreds of years before Moses with his regulations on the quality of sacrificial animals.

The quote where Jacob makes Joseph promise not to bury him in Egypt is from Genesis 47, verse 29. Putting one's hand under the thigh of another may have indicated submission to that person's authority.

CHAPTER 9

THE PARABLE OF TWO SONS

To the religious leaders of his time, Jesus told this story:

A certain man had two sons, and he came to the first and said, "Son, go work today in my vineyard."

He answered and said, "I will not," but afterward he repented and went.

And he came to the second, and said likewise. And he answered and said, "I go, sir," and went not.

Whether of them twain did the will of his father?

They [the chief priests and the elders of the people] say unto him [Jesus], The first.

Jesus saith unto them, Verily I say unto you, That the publicans and the harlots go into the kingdom of God before you. For John came unto you in the way of righteousness, and ye believed him not: but the publicans and the harlots believed him: and ye, when ye had seen it, repented not afterward, that ye might believe him.

John, often called John the Baptist, was baptizing people as a sign of their repentance.

The Father

The father in this story put up with the disrespectful manner in which the first son responded. He hadn't addressed his father as "sir" whereas the second son did. Nowadays, a son seldom addresses his father as "sir," but he might flatly refuse to obey. In those days, however, a Jewish son answering in that disrespectful way would be considered rebellious.

According to the Law of Moses, a stubborn and rebellious son should be stoned to death. The parents were to tell the elders of the town about it, "and all the men of his city shall stone him with stones, that he die."

Executing a rebellious child is a severe punishment, but probably few boys were stoned (killed by stoning). The threat was meant to induce them to change their ways.

A proverb of Solomon reads, "Withhold not correction from the child, for if thou beatest him with the rod, he shall not die. Thou shalt beat him with the rod, and shalt deliver his soul from hell."

"Hell," in this proverb, is the translation of the Hebrew *sheol*. The word suggests something worse than an ignoble or premature death, though the proverb could merely mean that a rebellious son, on being corrected and repenting, would be saved from the decreed death for rebellious sons.

If the father in the parable of the two sons is representative of our heavenly Father, he demonstrates mercy. He doesn't reprimand the disrespectful son.

What the father asked of his son was reasonable. Working in the vineyard could not be called slave labour although there may have been slaves or hired hands also working in the vineyard. If other workers saw a son working hard, they would be inspired to work hard also.

On the other hand, the vineyard may have been on a smaller scale, part of the family garden. All family members who could work were expected to work in it. And young people need to learn how to work.

The First Son

The fact that Jesus compared the first son to cheating tax collectors suggests that what he was doing instead of going to work in the vineyard might have been something not so good.

He was probably not involved with the collection of taxes. Tax collectors in those days were collecting for the Romans, a government the Jews despised. If there were loopholes in the tax laws, the tax collectors may not have advised their clients, but pocketed the extra money themselves.

Actually, two thousand years ago, tax collectors weren't that sophisticated. A tax collector might have lurked on the edge of a busy road, checking passers-by. Perhaps those who had already passed him warned oncoming travellers. Rather than an audible warning, a rapid blinking of the eyes may have been sufficient.

Whatever the first son may have been doing, he repented and did instead what his father wanted. It may not have been fear of getting stoned that caused him to change his mind. It may have been a realization that his father was thinking of the wellbeing of his family. As a family they could enjoy the fruit of their labour.

It's not the point of the story, but the son probably didn't wait until the last hour of the working day before going to work in the vineyard. And when he worked, he probably conscientiously pruned the vines or picked the grapes or whatever he had been asked to do. Even if he started late and did a sloppy job, it was better than the second son who didn't work at all.

Starting work early in the morning is the better way to go about it when working outside in Israel. Afternoons during the summer can be uncomfortably hot. When I was volunteering on a kibbutz on Mount Carmel, Israel, I sometimes joined the crew working in the banana plantation at the base of the mountain. We began work at daybreak and had the afternoons off. That was less than an eight-hour workday, but we did work six days a week.

Part of the work in the banana plantation was pruning. We sliced off the suckers growing at the base of the banana plant. To keep them from growing again, we poured *neft* over the cut. Neft smelled just like kerosene. I later learned that neft *is* kerosene.

Actually, we volunteers and the younger kibbutzniks didn't work so hard. Our kibbutz was the first kibbutz in Israel to go bankrupt; it is no longer a kibbutz.

The Second Son

The Father first asked one son to work in the vineyard and then asked the other. The first son may have been older, but designating one son as the first and the other as the second was principally a way of distinguishing between them.

The second son answered his father in a respectful manner, but his subsequent inaction showed disrespect. There are people who say the right things but don't really mean what they say. The second son had the makings of a politician.

That son may have been simply lazy. A proverb states, "As vinegar to the teeth, and as smoke to the eyes, so is the sluggard to them that send him."

The son might have been in the habit of staying up late at night and sleeping in late in the morning. Perhaps, late into the evening, he was reading by lamplight the racy parts of Scripture. Perhaps he slept till noon the next day and then decided it was too hot to go to work in the vineyard. Sleeping in late, however, would have been more difficult two thousand years ago than it would be now because individuals at that time didn't have so much privacy.

I'm reminded of a family I knew living back of the Mount of Olives. They had built a large addition to their home, yet parents and children still slept together in the same bedroom.

Possibly, however, the son had his own room. Perhaps the room was somewhat messy as he wasn't in the habit of picking up after himself. Perhaps his mother had told him to clean up his room a day or two before his father asked him to work in the vineyard, but he hadn't got around to it.

The son thought, "First things first," so spent most of the day cleaning up his room. His excuse for not working in the vineyard was that he had to clean up his room.

The second son may have been procrastinating, living by his own timing rather than his father's. He planned to work in the vineyard eventually but had other priorities. Perhaps, if the work was pruning the vines, he thought it could be done just as well another day.

I myself have a tendency to procrastinate. We have fruit trees at the moment that are in need of pruning, but I prefer writing to pruning. I wonder what the pruning hooks looked like that they used millennia ago. They may have been like small sickles with more of a V shape than a curved shape.

My son, when procrastinating, would usually be playing computer games instead of doing his homework. The second son in this story might also have liked to play games.

A game played millennia ago that is still popular today is the mill game, otherwise known as nine men's morris. Perhaps the second son got too involved playing the mill game so didn't get around to working in the vineyard.

Some teenagers really enjoy taking their car out for a spin, or their motorbike or whatever. Perhaps the second son had bought a pre-owned donkey and was testing it out.

Perhaps the second son kept busy doing things *related* to working in the vineyard. Grapes were often trampled in the winepress by young women. Perhaps he was rounding up some pretty young women to trample the grapes once they were harvested.

Perhaps the second son attached so little obligation to his promise that he forgot all about it. Or he remembered about it so late in the day that it wasn't worth going to work in the vineyard.

Perhaps the second son decided not to go to work in the vineyard after hearing that his brother had been asked to go but had refused. He thought it unfair that he should work while his brother was playing, or whatever his brother was doing instead of working in the vineyard.

Young people often think they are treated unfairly. I remember, as a young child, staying at my grandparents' place which bordered a creek. I wanted to sail to the sea. When no one was looking, I got a washtub and set off down the creek. However, there wasn't much water in the creek so the washtub got hung up on the stones of the creek bed. When getting out of the washtub to get a stick with which to push myself off the stones, the tub tipped and I got wet. That wasn't a problem. The problem was that my grandfather saw me and took the tub away.

I resented my grandfather squashing my adventurous spirit. It wasn't until sixteen years later, when I was twenty years old, that I was able to set out on my own to explore the world.

RELIGIOUS LEADERS

Jesus compared the religious leaders to the second son. The suggestion is that the religious leaders actually knew in the backs of their minds what God wanted them to do, but instead did what they wanted to do. We don't know whether the father punished the second son for his disobedience, but Jesus indicated eternal punishment for self-righteous religious leaders.

> Ye serpents, ye generation of vipers, how can ye escape the damnation of hell?

Even before Jesus upbraided the religious leaders, John the Baptist condemned them in similar words.

> O generation of vipers, who hath warned you to flee from the wrath to come?

Some religious leaders today may have a similar attitude to the religious leaders of Jesus' time. They busy themselves with religious activities, catering to their congregants. They may seem to be doing good, but only the Lord judges accurately what is good and what is not so good.

Breaking a promise, as the second son did, is worse than refusing to promise. On reading suggested ordination vows, I guess that few pastors live up to such a high standard. It would be good to aspire to high standards, but consistently failing to do so, and failing to repent for not doing so, is not good.

"Be ye perfect," Jesus said. That is the ultimate high standard. Perhaps he was reminding us of our failure to live consistently according to God's laws.

The second son and the religious leaders, simply by not doing what was expected of them, were doing wrong. There are sins of omission as well as sins of commission.

Jesus illustrated the sin of omission by telling a story of a servant who knew what his master wanted and another servant who didn't know.

> And that servant, which knew his lord's will, and prepared not himself, neither did according to his will, shall be beaten with many stripes. But he that knew not, and did commit things worthy of stripes, shall be beaten with few stripes.

This suggests degrees of punishment in hell. If there are varying rewards in heaven, there could also be varying degrees of punishment in hell.

Applying this to knowing what God wants us to do, there is value in studying Scripture only if a person applies what he has learned. If someone knows what to do but doesn't do it, the consequences are worse than for someone who didn't know what to do in the first place.

Jesus' brother James also wrote about the sin of omission. "Therefore to him that knoweth to do good, and doeth it not, to him it is sin."

We know, if we are honest with ourselves, what good we can do. We can help our neighbours, encouraging them to live in a righteous manner. We are not to help our neighbours, of course, in their wrongdoing.

I admit to having helped an employer, and in another case a friend, in wrongdoing. With the employer, I excused myself, telling myself that it was all part of the job. I didn't work for that employer for long. With the friend, I wanted to maintain the friendship. In that case, the friendship hasn't endured.

I admit to the sin of omission. Knowing the good that I could do, I have shirked responsibility. I haven't fulfilled the promises that I've made to the Lord. May the Lord be merciful.

Endnotes on Chapter 9

One of Jesus' followers, Matthew, recorded the parable of two sons, and was the only one of the Gospel writers to do so. Incidentally, he was a former tax collector. The parable is recorded in Matthew 21, verses 28 to 30, and Jesus' interaction with the religious leaders in verses 31 and 32.

Jesus' cousin John, often called John the Baptist, told the religious leaders to produce fruit in keeping with repentance. (Matt. 3:8, and Luke 3:8)

Those with sufficient food and clothing should share what they have with the needy. Government officials should not overcharge. Those in authority should not harass anybody, and workers should be content with their pay. See Luke 3, verses 11 to 14.

Deuteronomy 21, verses 18 to 21, instructs parents on how to deal with a stubborn and rebellious son. He should be executed. The quote is part of verse 21.

The quote about disciplining a child is Proverbs 23, verses 13 and 14.

The proverb about laziness is Proverbs 10, verse 26.

Jesus called the religious leaders a generation of vipers. (Matt. 23:33)

John the Baptist also called them a generation of vipers. The quote is part of Matthew 3, verse 7.

Jesus said, "Be ye therefore perfect, even as your Father which is in heaven is perfect" (Matt. 5:48).

He was quoting the Lord's instruction to Moses, "Speak unto all the congregation of the children of Israel, and say unto them, Ye shall be holy: for I the LORD your God am holy" (Lev. 19:2).

"Holy" is how the King James translators translated the Hebrew word. (I believe Jesus was quoting the Hebrew text. I doubt he was speaking Greek.)

The Greek word that is translated *perfect* can mean *mature*.

Jesus' parable of a servant who knew his master's will and another who didn't is in Luke 12. The quote is verse 47 and part of verse 48.

The quote about the sin of omission is from James 4, verse 17.

CHAPTER 10

Rash Wishes

"I wish by God…"

The Israelites

When the Israelites were travelling through the wilderness of Sin, they complained about the monotony of their diet. They remembered with nostalgia the variety of food they had eaten in Egypt, not appreciating the manna that the Lord provided for them in the wilderness. They complained to Moses and Aaron, "Would to God we had died by the hand of the LORD in the land of Egypt, when we sat by the flesh pots, and when we did eat bread to the full."

They remembered the good life in Egypt and forgot the hardships under slavery. They had selective memory.

The Israelites got their wish for meat in a seemingly miraculous manner.

> And there went forth a wind from the LORD, and
> brought quails from the sea, and let them fall by the

camp, as it were a day's journey on this side, and as it were a day's journey on the other side, round about the camp, and as it were two cubits high [about three feet in height] upon the face of the earth. And the people stood up all that day, and all that night, and all the next day, and they gathered the quails: he that gathered least gathered ten homers: and they spread them all abroad for themselves round about the camp. And while the flesh was yet between their teeth, ere it was chewed, the wrath of the LORD was kindled against the people, and the LORD smote the people with a very great plague.

The plague was the Lord's punishment for the Israelites' rash wish. It also seems to be connected to the eating of the quail. Perhaps it was salmonella poisoning, although that usually doesn't result in death. Also, the timing of the plague, "while the flesh was yet between their teeth, ere [before] it was chewed," wouldn't allow for poisoning.

Roast quail is delicious. There was a period in my life when I was short of money. That meant being short of food. I wished for a nice roast chicken or something like that. A quail flew into a window pane of the house in which I was staying. I rushed out, caught it while it was still stunned, wrung its neck, plucked it, cleaned it, cooked it, and ate it. That wasn't kosher. I should have slit its throat instead of wringing its neck.

The Israelites also complained when faced with the prospect of fighting to possess the promised land. They listened to the report of those returning from spying out the land. Ten of the spies had given a bad report, saying that although the land was bountiful, the people living there were powerful and their towns were large and fortified. They had even seen giants there.

Then the Israelites protested against Moses and Aaron, "Would God that we had died in the land of Egypt! or would God we had died in this wilderness!"

Their wish to die in the wilderness came true for almost all of them twenty years old or older who were numbered in the census. The censuses, whenever they took place, were only of men twenty years old or older. Twenty years old was of military age.

Thus it could be that many women who were twenty years old or older when they were turned back from entering the promised land did eventually enter it forty years later. Grandmothers were needed to help look after the families and livestock while the men were at war.

A sense of being needed does help people strive to continue living. Even today, women generally live longer than men. They feel they need to stick around to direct the affairs of the men.

The Israelites later complained when they had no water to drink, "Would God that we had died when our brethren died before the LORD!"

They were referring to Korah's rebellion when the earth opened up and swallowed Korah and his followers. Fire from the Lord burned up men who were offering incense, and many Israelites died of a plague. The Israelites weren't thankful for being spared from the calamity that befell Korah and his followers, and from the following plague in which many thousands had died.

Being thirsty might seem to be sufficient reason to complain. In the wilderness of Sin, the Lord was providing food in the form of manna, but seemed slack in providing yet more vital water. Sometimes the Lord's timing of when to provide for our needs is different from our timing.

Two Leaders

Joshua was one of only two men of this older generation whom the Lord allowed to enter the promised land. Even he, however, had his moments of reconsideration. When the men of Ai defeated some of the Israelites, Joshua remarked, "Would to God we had been content, and dwelt on the other side Jordan!" He regretted crossing to the west bank.

The Lord showed him what the problem was; one of the men, Achan, had taken some of the spoils of Jericho. All of the spoils were supposed to be devoted to the Lord. When Achan's sin was dealt with, the Israelites dealt with the town of Ai.

Another prominent leader, King David, also made a rash wish. His son Absalom had led an insurrection against him, but in a battle in which thousands died, Absalom was killed. King David mourned, "O my son Absalom, my son, my son Absalom! would God I had died for thee, O Absalom, my son, my son!"

King David's military commander, Joab, rebuked him, saying "I perceive, that if Absalom had lived, and all we had died this day, then it had pleased thee well."

King David realized he was being ungrateful and stopped his public mourning for his son. Wishing his own death instead of his son's was wrong, but despite some wayward ways, God could still call David "a man after my own heart."

THE APOSTLE PAUL

A scriptural example of someone wishing something bad upon himself is the apostle Paul wishing that he himself were accursed instead of his kinsmen. He was emphasizing his concern for the Jews. Although he called himself an apostle to the Gentiles, he also had a strong desire to see his fellow Jews accept Jesus as their Messiah.

The attitude with which a person makes the wish is important. In the apostle Paul's case, he had the right attitude, believing that there are eternal consequences for rejecting Jesus. A person's attitude toward Jesus reflects an attitude toward God who sent Jesus to save people from condemnation.

Wishing something bad about oneself is usually wrong. The motive is hate rather than, as in the apostle Paul's case, love. Self-hatred is not humility. It does not promote love for others. Wishing can turn into actually harming ourselves. If the harm is self-inflicted bodily injury, it is obviously not good, but we can also harm ourselves in a multitude of other ways.

During my unhappy teenage years, I sometimes wished I were dead. It would have been worse if I had actually said out loud, "I wish I were dead!" Verbal statements seem to have more effect than mere thoughts.

Faults and Frailties

Scripture records the human frailties of characters of old. When they made a rash promise or a rash wish, it could be recorded because they had expressed themselves.

I don't emphasize my wishes with an oath, but have at times felt the same way as the Israelites remembering the good life in Egypt. Before getting married, I was freer to follow my fantasies. I remember the good life being single, but forget the bad times. That, again, is selective memory.

Saying that, as a single person, I was freer to follow my fantasies suggests that I was following my own whims rather than seeking the Lord's will for my life. It would have been a lot better to have been wholeheartedly following the Lord.

It is also wrong to remember with nostalgia the better physical and mental condition that I had in my youth. Then there are the lost opportunities. When I dream of what might have been, it suggests that I'm not appreciating my present situation.

If daydreaming is rash wishing, then I have been guilty for decades and still succumb to the temptation. As a teenager back on the farm, my brother and I dug a new outside toilet hole as the old one was full. I dug deeper and deeper, loading the earth in a bucket which my brother hauled up with a rope. I dreamed of digging so deep we stuck oil, but my stepfather stopped us. The hole was deep enough for the intended purpose.

Decades later, after my stepfather sold the farm, drillers struck oil about a hundred yards from that toilet hole. It was the largest oil-producing well in southern Alberta.

To Be a Star

Teenage boys often want to excel in some sport or other. I didn't excel, though I dreamt of being a baseball or hockey star. Actually, one season, I was the star of our school football (gridiron) team. Because of the limited number of boys to make up the team, I was included although I was probably the smallest player on the team. But I was a fast runner. I made the only touchdown our team made all season.

If not impressing people with my athletic ability, I dreamt of impressing them with my reasoning ability. Velocity is distance divided by time. If space is expanding, that means that the distance through which light travels is increasing. But, since the speed of light is said to be a constant, might it also mean that time is dilating? None of my classmates were interested in my speculations.

If not in sports or in physics, how could I impress the young ladies? Fashion perhaps. I started the fad of wearing torn jeans. I did try to save a good pair of jeans for school, but after returning home from school often neglected to change out of my school jeans before doing the farm chores. Consequently, the two or three pairs of jeans that I had were often torn or patched. My mother patched my jeans. Imagine nowadays asking a teenager wearing torn jeans, "Couldn't you get your mom to patch them?"

Other boys in our high school often wore dress pants unless they were planning on practicing some sport or other during lunch break. I persisted in establishing the torn jean fad.

My fashion statement didn't impress the young ladies. What might have impressed them was having a car at my disposal. However, I was seldom allowed to borrow the family car. I dreamt of designing a vehicle something like a batmobile that could also fly.

The community where I lived didn't have a hall suitable for dancing, but neighbouring communities did. The one time that I went to a dance, I hung around the wall watching others dance. A classmate's mother had given ballroom dance lessons to whomever wanted to come, but I didn't have the opportunity to go to the lessons. At that time, dancers making movements that dancers make nowadays would have been considered weird.

Girls are not attracted to shy and insecure guys. The following story reminds me of myself:

A guy was given advice as to how to make conversation at a social event. Ask questions such as "Are you married? Do you have children?"

So, while making conversation with an attractive young lady, he asked, "Are you married?"

"No," she responded.

"Do you have children?"

Cool Dudes

Women are attracted to cool dudes. I remember a situation when I was volunteering on the kibbutz on Mount Carmel. I attempted to act cool in the presence of some young ladies. But I was having difficulty getting the cap off my bottle of beer when there was no bottle opener handy. The young ladies found me amusing rather than cool.

Later, after joining church and ministry teams, I appeared cool to spiritually minded ladies. In fact, I attracted one lady sufficiently enough that she agreed to marry me. But she no longer considers me cool. My life lacks luster. Perhaps I should resume hang-gliding or paragliding.

Self-confident, competent men attract women. If a man has the advantage of being good-looking, or is popular in the field of sports or music or theatre, he might even be idolized. If such a man shows an interest in a beautiful young woman, he could easily take advantage of her.

A genuine interest in another person, with a desire for the other person's well-being, is called love. During our time here on earth, we should be developing our ability to love. I already discussed in a previous chapter the command, "Love thy neighbour as thyself." That is not a command for me to love a particularly attractive neighbour lady.

Thinking about making a good impression on others, I remember another incident on the kibbutz when I failed to make the desired impression. I'll first have to give background details.

On the kibbutz, I worked mostly with concrete. My boss liked my work so he kept me busy around the kibbutz whereas other volunteers often had a greater variety of jobs.

Years after leaving the kibbutz, I returned for a visit. My former boss was concerned that contractors who were laying the concrete foundations for something were not doing a proper job. He asked me to go over and examine their work. I would pretend to be a construction specialist. So I went over to where the contractors were working. Their boss, who could speak English, struck up a conversation with me. It soon became apparent that I didn't know much about concrete foundations. When he asked me, I had to admit that my former boss wanted me to pose as a construction specialist. My former boss's wish to get a better concrete foundation was rather rash.

How can we make a good impression on God? Good works may help, but we can't earn salvation. While seeking what the Lord's will might be for our lives, it would be good to keep busy doing good works. We shouldn't look back with nostalgia to good times, not appreciating how the Lord is blessing us in the present.

Life has not been as I dreamed it might be, but I have to admit that the Lord has blessed me with, among other things, a comparatively good wife and son.

ENDNOTES ON CHAPTER 10

The wilderness of Sin is also called the desert of Zin (Num. 20:3). When travelling through it, the Israelites complained that they didn't have enough to eat, so the Lord gave them manna for food. Even that didn't stop their complaining,

"Who shall give us flesh to eat? We remember the fish, which we did eat in Egypt freely; the cucumbers, and the melons, and the leeks, and the onions, and the garlick. But now our soul is dried away; there is nothing at all, beside this manna, before our eyes" (part of Num. 11:4–6).

"Would to God we had died by the hand of the LORD in the land of Egypt, when we sat by the flesh pots, and when we did eat bread to the full" (part of Ex. 16:3).

The Lord provided quail for the Israelites to eat. Many Christian translations say the quail were piled upon the ground, but many Jewish translations say the quail were flying above the ground at a certain height (making it easy for people to catch them). The account of the quail is in Numbers 11, verses 31 and 32. Verse 33 tells about the plague.

Fearful of the giants they would have to fight to conquer the promised land, the Israelites complained, "Would God that we had died in the land of Egypt! or would God we had died in this wilderness!" (part of Num. 14:2).

At Meribah, the Israelites complained again, "Would God that we had died when our brethren died before the LORD!" (part of Num. 20:3).

The account of Korah's rebellion and subsequent punishments can be found in Numbers 16.

When some Israelites were defeated by the men of Ai, Joshua regretted crossing to the west bank. "Would to God we had been content, and dwelt on the other side Jordan" (part of Josh. 7:7).

King David grieved for his son, "O my son Absalom, my son, my son Absalom! would God I had died for thee, O Absalom, my son, my son!" (part of 2 Sam. 18:33).

Joab rebuked him, "I perceive that if Absalom had lived and all we had died this day, then it had pleased thee well" (part of 2 Sam. 19:6).

In 1 Samuel 13, verse 14, the Lord refers to David as a man after his own heart. In Acts 13, verse 22, Stephen also recounts this.

The apostle Paul wrote, "For I could wish that myself were accursed from Christ for my brethren, my kinsmen according to the flesh" (Rom. 9:3).

CHAPTER 11

BRASH CONDUCT

Young Moses was concerned for his own
kinsmen, but he acted rashly.

And it came to pass in those days, when Moses
was grown, that he went out unto his brethren, and
looked on their burdens; and he spied an Egyptian
smiting an Hebrew, one of his brethren. And he
looked this way and that way, and when he saw that
there was no man, he slew the Egyptian, and hid
him in the sand.

Killing the Egyptian when he thought no one was looking, and
hiding the body in the sand, wasn't the best way to begin setting his
people free from Egyptian slavery. Many years later he did lead his
people to freedom. God's timing is best.

BAD TIMING

When the Israelites first approached the promised land,
they feared going in to fight the inhabitants and
even considered returning to Egypt. Due to their

faithlessness, they were told that all the men except Joshua and Caleb were destined to wander in the wilderness and die there. On hearing of their punishment, they changed their mind and entered the land, but were chased back by the inhabitants. They had missed the Lord's timing.

Another instance of wrong timing is that of a man gathering firewood on the Sabbath.

> And all the congregation brought him without the camp, and stoned him with stones, and he died; as the LORD commanded Moses.

This is the commandment about not working on the Sabbath:

> Remember the sabbath day, to keep it holy. Six days shalt thou labour, and do all thy work.
> But the seventh day is the sabbath of the LORD thy God; in it thou shalt not do any work, thou, nor thy son, nor thy daughter, thy manservant, nor thy maidservant, nor thy cattle, nor thy stranger that is within thy gates.

The seventh day is Saturday, but since Constantine, most Christians have observed Sunday as the Sabbath. According to Nehemiah, working on the Sabbath profanes it. Working included treading grapes, bringing in sheaves, transporting goods, and buying and selling goods. Might there be any profanity in buying and selling on Sunday?

Jesus implied that it was all right for people to do *necessary* work on the Sabbath. Speaking to the religious leaders of his time, Jesus questioned, "Have ye not read in the law, how that on the Sabbath days the priests in the temple profane the Sabbath, and are blameless?"

Nowadays, most Christian priests and pastors officiate in their churches on Sunday. Then many of them take Monday as their day of rest.

Necessary work on the farm where I lived as a teenager included milking the cows and feeding the pigs and suchlike chores. During haying season, we sometimes stacked hay on a Sunday if there was a threat of rain the next day.

Since that time, I had a job where I was required to work weekends. There were extra duties that those on shift could do when they had time. On Saturdays and Sundays, I seldom found time to do those extras. I wasn't sure which day was the Sabbath. That was my excuse to myself, anyway.

TEMPTATION

Israel's last judge, Samson, was careless in his conduct. He shouldn't have gotten involved with those Philistine women, no matter how beautiful they might have been.

On the way to his wedding party, he collected some honey from a beehive in the carcass of a dead lion. Thinking of bees getting robbed of their honey, it could be that bee stings to someone like Samson were no worse than mosquito bites to the average person.

At the party, Samson proposed a riddle for the Philistines to solve. By badgering him, Samson's bride got him to tell her the answer to his riddle. She told the Philistines and they told Samson the answer, which was to do with honey from a lion. Realizing his bride had told them, Samson stormed out.

The best-known story of Samson is the one of him and Delilah. He had fallen in love with another pagan woman. She pressed him to know the secret of his great strength, having been offered a large sum of money by the Philistines if she would aid in his capture.

Samson's superhuman strength was tied to his keeping of Nazarite vows. Samson told Delilah a couple of ways by which he might be bound, but when she bound him, he broke free.

Delilah kept pleading with Samson, so he finally told her about the Nazarite vow never to shave his head. He hadn't learned the lesson from when he revealed the answer to his riddle to his former honey.

While he slept with his head in her lap, Delilah got a man to shave his head. When he awoke, he found that his strength had left him. The Philistines seized him, gouged out his eyes, and bound him with shackles.

Without eyes, it wouldn't have mattered whether Samson had hair hanging over his face. Previously, such as when he was slaying Philistines with the jawbone of a donkey, Samson must have tied his hair back so it wouldn't impair his vision. Perhaps he tied it back in a ponytail.

PRESUMPTION

King Saul, although not qualified to do such a thing, offered a sacrifice to seek the Lord's favour for a pending battle with the Philistines. He had been waiting for Samuel the prophet to come, but with the delay, his fighting men were deserting him.

Just as he finished sacrificing, Samuel arrived. King Saul tried to excuse his actions,

I saw that the people were scattered from me, and that thou camest not within the days appointed. Therefore said I, The Philistines will come down now upon me to Gilgal, and I have not made supplication unto the LORD. I forced myself therefore, and offered a burnt offering.

Samuel responded that because of King Saul's rash action he would not remain king. The fact that Samuel was late in coming was no excuse.

An unnamed prophet from Judah went to Bethel and prophesied against the irreligious system of worship that King Jeroboam had set up. On his way back to Judah an old prophet caught up to him and invited him to come home with him for a meal.

The prophet from Judah replied,

I may not return with thee, nor go in with thee; neither will I eat bread nor drink water with thee in this place; for it was said to me by the word of the LORD, Thou shalt eat no bread nor drink water there.

The old prophet, however, deceptively persuaded the prophet from Judah to return with him. He ate bread and drank water in the old prophet's home.

On his way back to Judah a lion killed him. The consequence probably would have been similar if, instead of eating bread and drinking water, he had eaten meat and drunk wine.

IRREVERENCE

Religious leaders can act irreverently, treating sacred things as common. Ezekiel prophesied about the land,

> Her priests have violated my law, and have profaned mine holy things; they have put no difference between the holy and profane.

The pastor of a Jerusalem church where I was caretaker sometimes finished the leftover grape juice after communion if I didn't get to it first. He didn't seem to drink it so reverently. Perhaps there wasn't anything sacred about the grape juice.

Another time I lived in a monastery near Bet Shemesh. The priest there did drink the leftover wine more reverently, and there was a lot of leftover wine after Mass.

We generally don't think of some food being holier than others (besides Swiss cheese being holier than other types of cheese) but we are profaning holy things by taking communion irreverently. The apostle Paul wrote,

> Wherefore whosoever shall eat this bread, and drink this cup of the Lord, unworthily, shall be guilty of the body and blood of the Lord. For he that eateth and drinketh unworthily, eateth and drinketh damnation to himself, not discerning the Lord's body. For this cause many are weak and sickly among you, and many sleep.

Partaking of communion in an unworthy manner causing a person to "sleep" does not suggest boredom causing sleepiness. "Sleep" in this case is a euphemism for "die." The Lord takes profanity seriously. There can be bodily effects on the person profaning holy things.

The apostle Paul instructed the Church in Rome about eating meat. Many of the believers had emerged from paganism, having participated in pagan practices such as sacrificing to a god. The barbecued meat was then eaten. Some new believers felt uneasy about eating meat that had been sacrificed to idols. More mature believers could reason that there was nothing wrong with the meat itself. The apostle Paul wrote,

> He that eateth, eateth to the Lord, for he giveth God thanks; and he that eateth not, to the Lord he eateth not, and giveth God thanks.

Addressing particularly the more mature believers, he wrote,

> It is good neither to eat flesh, nor to drink wine, nor any thing whereby thy brother stumbleth, or is offended, or is made weak.

For the sake of unity in the church, they should refrain from eating meat if it bothered a brother, and probably also if it bothered a sister in the Lord. Also included was drinking wine. The apostle Paul didn't mention beer.

Possibly causing someone to fall into temptation, however, is a good reason to abstain from drinking alcohol. That was the reason given by the administration of the Bible school that I attended for requiring all graduates to abstain from alcohol for the rest of their lives.

What Not To Do

The reborners with whom I associated as a teenager were somewhat legalistic. For example, they wouldn't go shopping on Sunday. Few stores back then were open on Sunday anyway. Neither did we go out to eat in a restaurant after the Sunday morning service, as we didn't have money to spend like that.

Playing sports on Sunday was frowned upon, though we weren't too strict about refraining from enjoying ourselves. I heard this story:

A pastor of a church in Scotland lived a short distance from the church. He lived beside the same river as the church. One Sunday in winter he decided to skate to church rather than walk.

The elders of the church thought that he was out of place to have skated to church. In the discussion about whether their pastor had sinned, it boiled down to whether he had *enjoyed* skating.

Culture seems to determine what we consider to be right or wrong. Some other Christians with whom I associated complained of inconsistencies. They were visiting a church in the southern United States. They wore jackets and ties to church, but in the afternoon they were playing ball on the church grounds while wearing shorts. A church member approached them, telling them it was improper to wear shorts on Sunday. He had a cigarette in his hand.

SEEKING SIGNS

Ancient divination methods may seem rather crude to us now. One method amongst Babylonians, even extending to the Romans, was examining the liver of a slaughtered sheep or goat. The colour and configurations of the liver would direct them in their decision-making. Nowadays, some people read Tarot cards or horoscopes.

I remember a situation where seeking a sign didn't seem to me to be a good thing to do. When I was a young believer, three other young men visited me in my little flat (apartment). We were discussing spiritual topics late into the evening. I wanted to go to bed because the next morning I had to get up early to go to work. They were deciding whether to go home or simply crash at my place for the night.

They decided to seek a sign as to whether they should stay. If the floor creaked, they would stay. I stayed as still as possible in case movement caused the floor to creak. But then it creaked! They stayed the night.

I got through the day okay, but that evening I fell asleep during the evening course that I was taking. On subsequent evenings I also fell asleep right there in the classroom. I ended up dropping the course.

INCONSIDERATION

An example comes to mind of inconsideration. When I was walking in an area of Jerusalem, the noise of many cars honking drew my attention to a bus stopped in the middle of the road blocking all traffic behind it. It was stopped where the street made a turn. Parked on the turn was a car. The bus couldn't make the turn past the car.

In front of the bus was a man waving to the bus driver that he would direct him in maneuvering around the parked car. The bus driver purposefully ignored him. Bus drivers driving Jerusalem's narrow streets know to the centimetre where the side of their bus will be on any turn.

Eventually a man carrying a falafel came to the parked car. There was a popular falafel stand nearby. The man got into the car and drove off. The bus continued on its way. The honking diminished to its usual volume.

DISHONESTY

Inconveniencing others is inconsiderate, but defrauding others is sinning. Moses ruled that false weights should not be used in a balance scale. "Thou shalt not have in thy bag divers weights, a great and a small."

I already explained in a previous chapter that *divers* has the accent on the second syllable. While it is true that scuba divers use weights, the context doesn't allow for scuba-diving weights. When checking the context, I found the preceding couple of verses to be also about rash conduct and the prescribed consequence.

> When men strive together one with another, and
> the wife of the one draweth near for to deliver her
> husband out of the hand of him that smiteth him,
> and putteth forth her hand, and taketh him by the

secrets: Then thou shalt cut off her hand, thine eye shall not pity her.

Another translation, instead of "taketh him by the secrets" has "seizes him by the private parts." I can't illustrate this with a story from when I lived in Israel, but I'll tell a story about divers weights.

I was buying bananas in a small market in the Christian Quarter of the Old City of Jerusalem. They required weighing so the vendor weighed them on a balance scale right beside where he was sitting. I noticed that his stomach was touching the pan with the weights in it, so I made him reweigh the bananas. They didn't weigh as much as he pretended they did.

In that case, the weights themselves in the balance scale were accurate, so strictly speaking, he was not disobeying the letter of the Law. But he was definitely disobeying the spirit of the Law. It must have taken quite a bit of practice to ease his stomach against the pan at the precise moment to hold the scale balanced.

ENDNOTES ON CHAPTER 11

The passage where Moses murders the Egyptian is Exodus 2, verses 11 and 12.

The account of the Israelites missing the Lord's timing is in Numbers 14.

The account of the Sabbath breaker is in Numbers 15, verses 32 to 36. Verse 36 is quoted.

The commandment about observing the Sabbath is in Exodus 20, verses 8 to 11 (also Deut. 5:12–15). The quote is Exodus 20, verses 8 to 10.

Nehemiah considered working on the Sabbath to be profaning the Sabbath. See Nehemiah 13, verses 15 to 17.

By his question, Jesus explained that it wasn't profaning the Sabbath to do necessary work on that day. "Or have ye not read in the law, how that on the Sabbath days the priests in the temple profane the Sabbath, and are blameless?" (Matt. 12:5).

The story of Sampson can be found in Judges, chapters 13 to 16. Israelites were forbidden to marry unbelieving foreigners (Ex. 34:16 and Deut. 7:3). Stipulations for a Nazarite are in Judges 6.

The account of King Saul offering a burnt sacrifice is in 1 Samuel 13. The quote is part of verse 11 and all of verse 12.

The story of the unnamed prophet from Judah who went to Bethel is in 1 Kings 13. The quote is parts of verses 16 and 17.

In Ezekiel 22, verse 26, Ezekiel wrote about priests profaning holy things.

The apostle Paul advised reverence when partaking of the Lord's supper. The quote is from 1 Corinthians 11, verses 27 to 30.

The quote about eating or not eating meat is part of verse 6 of Romans 14. The quote about not eating meat or drinking wine or any suchlike thing is verse 21 of Romans 14.

Ezekiel describes King Nebuchadnezzar divining during his military campaign. One of the signs giving him direction came from examining the liver of a slaughtered animal. (Ezek. 21:21)

Moses instructed, "Thou shalt not have in thy bag divers weights, a great and a small" (Deut. 25:13).

The preceding couple of verses (Deut. 25:11–12) are about a woman's possible rash conduct and the prescribed consequences.

CHAPTER 12

SELF-ASSERTION

A rich man, after gaining yet more riches, said to himself,

> "Soul, thou hast much goods laid up for many years;
> take thine ease, eat, drink, and be merry."
> But God said unto him, "Thou fool, this night
> thy soul shall be required of thee: then whose shall
> those things be, which thou hast provided?"

God condemned him as a fool for considering only his own physical well-being. It is not necessarily wrong to save up for retirement, but we do need to consider the needs of others.

ASPIRATIONS

It is not necessarily wrong for a boy to aspire to be rich when he grows up, but money can become an idol replacing an appreciation of God. If, however, the boy felt deprived and vowed that he wouldn't be poor when he grew up, that can be an inner impulse that influences him negatively. He may get rich, but he may also become a workaholic, neglecting his family.

Vows we make to ourselves are sometimes called "inner vows." They are usually not spoken, and may not even be remembered if they were made when we were young. Even when not remembered, however, they settle in the subconscious and influence the way we think and feel. Good vows and bad vows are like seeds sown, which some day produce more of the same. The apostle Paul said, "Whatsoever a man soweth, that shall he also reap."

Because children don't have the capabilities or opportunities that adults have, they resolve to do something or not to do something when they get older. Vows to themselves are often made when they are sulking, angry, or afraid.

Rabbis say that the vow of a young child is considered to be no vow. That means that the spoken vow of a young child should not be taken seriously. However, if the child is hurt, resentful, or fearful, even unspoken vows lodge in the child's subconscious.

A child might repeat, "Sticks and stones may break my bones, but names will never hurt me." That is not true, however. A child is deeply affected by other people's attitudes.

A girl in elementary school was teased because of her red hair. (It could be that the girls teasing her were actually jealous.) She resolved to dye her hair another colour as soon as her mother would let her.

As a teenager, she dyed her hair blue or pink or green–any colour but red. This was despite her mother telling her that she looked nicer with her natural red hair. She didn't even remember the vow of her childhood.

Children may not be able to do much about the condition they dislike, but they can resolve to rectify it when able. If they feel deprived of material things, when they grow up they might have an inordinate desire for material possessions.

A more serious deprivation is a lack of love and affection. Children need lots of attention–the right kind of attention. If they feel a lack of love, there might later be an unhealthy desire for the approval of others. They might also go to the other extreme of rejecting any offer of love, isolating themselves from others.

An example of a woman being affected by her childhood

experience would be when she didn't get the attention she wanted from her father, or got the wrong kind of attention. After growing up, she might project the attitude that she had toward her father onto her husband.

As a child, I probably made a number of promises that I now don't even remember. However, I remember one promise because my grandmother reminded me of it when I was a teenager. She had found it amusing because of my praiseworthy first assertion followed by a disappointing add-on. My grandparents were non-smokers and teetotalers.

I had said, "I'm not going to smoke when I grow up…but I think I'll drink." And that's the way it's been.

During my unhappy teenage years, I must have made several promises to myself. After revealing how I felt about life, and being told that what I felt was so wrong, I probably promised never again to reveal my true feelings. Such vows can result in frozen emotions. Another promise may have been, "I'll get out of here as soon as I can!" Running away from home, however, wasn't an option.

I stuck it out till my late teens when I left home for further education. And then I realized that most of my problems were within me, not just external. One of my frustrations living at home had been my stepfather's erratic decision-making. Interestingly, I can now stick it out when under erratic control *if I can leave when I choose*.

Decades later I was in a work situation where there was a difficult and erratic boss in one department. Employees refused to work under him. I was sent there as I was the type of guy who could take it. He and I got along fairly well and I learned a lot from the experience, particularly what *wouldn't* work.

It seems reasonable to want to get out of a bad situation such as the farm where I lived as a teenager. My motive, however, was self-interest rather than wanting to do what the Lord wanted me to do. Although this was before I had any interest in the Lord's will, promises that I made to myself back then seem to affect my relationship to the Lord now. Promises prompted by resentment hinder response to God's love.

An indication that vows of my youth still affect me is the frustration I feel over erratic control in family affairs. It is erratic control when one member of the family is permitted to make and receive phone calls on the Sabbath but another member of the family is *not* permitted to send or receive emails. And this was way back when both phone calls and emails were sent and received via the same copper line.

"Not to" promises to ourselves often result in our doing what we vowed not to do. Perhaps a resentful attitude toward those who controlled me in my youth prompted me, in a reverse manner, to put myself in the same situation. By focusing on a character fault in another person, our association with it is amplified. They say that a woman with a drunken father is more likely to marry a drunkard.

Some psychologists even suggest that the attitude a girl develops toward her father can affect her future husband. If she resented her father's drunkenness, she might actually *turn* her husband into a drunkard. It's an unconscious expectation that her husband will act in the same manner. The expectation then becomes a reality, just as seeds sown eventually produce more of the same. She reaps what has been sown.

Resentment is critical judgement. Jesus said,

> Judge not, that ye be not judged. For with what judgment ye judge, ye shall be judged: and with what measure ye mete, it shall be measured to you again.

Jesus was saying that if we judge others, we will be judged in the same manner. We will get what we didn't want.

We need to acknowledge that the resentments of our youth were wrong. Our appraisal of the situation may have been correct, but we were wrong to have judged critically. We need to renounce any negative inner vows we may have made.

When realizing that we are holding grudges, the longer we wait before repenting, the more difficult it is to actually do it. The longer we harbour unforgiveness, the more difficult it is to forgive.

"Good" Vows

Seemingly good vows might also negatively affect us. We strive in our own strength to achieve goals, but our goals may be different from what God has planned for us. Striving to live how we think God wants us to live is not good when we have a wrong concept of what God wants us to do. We may be involved in religious activities that are of no spiritual benefit.

"Not to" promises to ourselves are often made with a judgemental attitude, but in certain situations, a self-promise such as "I'll never do that again" could be a good promise. As a child, I had been warned not to lick metal railings in mid-winter. Children have ripped the skin of their tongues by jerking away when their tongues froze to the metal.

As a teenager, one cold day, I thought I would just touch the tip of my tongue to a metal railing. My tongue froze to it. I didn't jerk away but crouched there breathing heavily for many minutes. Before the metal warmed up enough to free my tongue, more than the tip of my tongue was stuck to the railing. I had a sore tongue for hours after. I'll never do that again!

But an "I'll never…" such as I heard my teenage son say, might bind him for life. Witnessing one of our domestic disputes, he said, "I'll never get married!" Years later when I reminded him of his vow, he didn't remember it, but he said he had little interest in getting married.

Then there are conditional vows such as "If I don't do___well, I'm a failure." (Fill in the blank.) A vow like that could keep a person from attempting something new. I'm reminded of a youth attempting water skiing. His younger brother managed to stay up on the skis after his first or second try. The older brother failed to stay up on the skis after his first or second try. He gave up trying to water ski.

Perfectionists take to the extreme the saying, "Whatever is worth doing, is worth doing well." Taking time to do a good job is okay, but if the time taken means neglecting doing something more important, then it's not okay. I remember a situation in Israel involving drip irrigation. (Israelis popularized drip irrigation.) An acquaintance had extended drip irrigation tubes to each individual flower. That was overkill (or overnurture) in my opinion. I myself have a tendency to get overly concerned about details so I shouldn't be too critical of others.

Timidity in public speaking may be the result of an inner vow. "If I fumble my words, I would be so embarrassed!" Of course, before speaking to a large audience, most people are apprehensive. But the other extreme of neglecting to prepare the speech before speaking is also not good.

Foolish Vows

In a previous chapter, I condensed one of Moses' directives, "If anyone utters a rash oath, when he realizes its foolishness, he must admit his guilt and make compensation for the sin he has committed."

In that case it was a voiced vow, but foolish unvoiced vows also need to be renounced. Such vows are often made in resentment, and resentment is sin. A person needs to admit the sin and ask the Lord for forgiveness. Similar to bad habits, vows may need to be renounced over and over again until broken.

A rash promise, even though no longer remembered, might prompt an irrational response. I heard of a test that a psychiatrist made on a patient. The patient had told him that he was allergic to roses. Before the next counselling session, the psychiatrist put a vase of *artificial* roses on his desk. When the patient came into the room, he saw the roses and manifested all the symptoms of an allergic reaction.

Perhaps he had a trauma in his youth in connection with roses. He liked a girl but was timid about approaching her. Finally, he built up enough courage to present her with a rose (picked from his neighbour's flower garden). She took it in her dainty little hand but then screamed, "I hate you! I hate you!" and ran off. She had pricked her finger on a thorn on the rose and thought that he had purposely given it to her as a joke. Perhaps he then promised to himself, "I'll never ever touch another rose. I *hate* roses."

Another reaction in another situation might be excessive anger. I still remember a pastor's inappropriate display of anger.

I was in a country school. During lunch break, some of us teenage boys were outside. Some girls were also outside, a distance away from us. One of the boys in our group decided to throw stones at the girls. They weren't in danger as they were far enough away that they could easily dodge the stones if the stones even reached that far. They were watching us.

Also watching us from a window in the parsonage, was the pastor of the nearby church. He rushed out and began throwing stones at the boy who had been throwing stones at the girls. The boy was rolling on the ground crying as the pastor stoned him.

Inappropriate displays of anger are often prompted by critical judgments. Perhaps the pastor, as a boy, had heard about Moses' law that stubborn and rebellious boys should be stoned to death. Perhaps he himself was stubborn and rebellious, but thought that stoning was too severe a punishment. He resolved, "I would never, ever stone anyone!" But judgmental resolutions have a strange way of causing a person to do what he resolved not to do.

It may not have been the inappropriate display of the pastor's anger that prompted me to distance myself from the church, but it didn't endear me to it. I now regret my brash conduct in some situations and my passivity in others.

I shouldn't criticize the pastor's inappropriate display of anger when I was acting not so sensibly myself. One of the stoned girls was particularly attractive and I was attracted to her. A while before the stoning incident, in order to attract her attention, I kicked her. That was inappropriate.

I tend to idolize beautiful young ladies. The beautiful young lady of my teenage years no doubt had faults but I didn't see any, except that she didn't show enough interest in me.

Since then, I have tended to withdraw, which would be a good thing if the sole result were a reduction in kicking. It's like building a wall around myself. But it keeps me from loving others and from receiving the love others try to show. It's like voluntary solitary confinement.

TRUE LOVE

What is love? The term "making love" may have little to do with true love. In the heat of the moment, a man might say things that he later regrets. I heard of a woman suing a man for breaking his promise.

The man argued that promises made during such moments shouldn't be binding.

How can we become genuinely loving? Shakespeare wrote, "Assume a virtue, if you have it not." In other words, adopt a virtue and act upon it although you may not feel it. This is not the same as believing we are loving because we perform charitable acts. It is focusing away from oneself.

The apostle Paul wrote, "For all the law is fulfilled in one word, even in this; Thou shalt love thy neighbour as thyself."

Evidently the apostle Paul wasn't much of a mathematician. I count seven words in English. In Greek it is six words and in Hebrew it is four. But it's true that we should love our neighbours. I have difficulty, I admit, with one of mine. And loving oneself? I have difficulty with that also.

As well as writing about loving our neighbours, the apostle Paul wrote, "Let love be without dissimulation." These days, we would say "without pretense" rather than "without dissimulation." Other translations put it in the positive such as "Let love be genuine" or "Let love be sincere."

How can we judge whether love is sincere? Objective analysis is easier. A situation in Israel comes to mind. A shifty-eyed stranger tried to befriend my boss's dog. It seemed obvious to me that his motive was not pure friendliness. He hoped that the dog would recognize him and not bark when he came to burgle the place. And the place did get burgled. Whether it was by him, I don't know.

Subjective analysis is more difficult. It means honest introspection–are we really loving? We might think good deeds should earn God's favour, but were they really done with a loving attitude? We shouldn't get absorbed with self. It is better to concentrate on helping others and let God do the judging.

According to Jesus, loving our neighbours is second to loving God. Jesus said, "Thou shalt love the Lord thy God with all thy heart, and with all thy soul, and with all thy mind."

Again, a situation in Israel comes to mind. A religious person with whom I associated spent a lot of time with religious activities but didn't seem to care much about the welfare of others. But I shouldn't judge.

Then there are stories that I heard of reclusive monks isolating themselves in order to devote themselves to prayer. One story was of a monk who used to live in a cave high up on a cliff near St. George Monastery in Wadi Qelt. With a rope, he would lower a bucket in which other monks would put food and water. Was he earning his keep? Prayer is work. Only God knows the effectiveness of his prayers.

Loving God would mean keeping promises. Some of the promises we made may have been rash. We can ask for forgiveness for making rash promises and make amends if need be. Other promises may have been good promises. We can ask for the Lord's help to remember and keep those promises.

We need to distinguish, however, between good promises and rash promises. A promise to become a missionary in some foreign land, for example, may not necessarily be a good promise. It may have been made more out of a desire to emulate another missionary. In a case such as this, it may be best to pray that the Lord forgive us for making the rash promise and help us to remember and keep more realistic promises, such as to serve the Lord wherever we are.

Even those averse to praying can alleviate inner conflicts by renouncing rash promises. If we are aware of a particular rash promise and want to revoke it, we could write on a piece of paper, "I release myself from my vow that___" (fill in the blank). Saying it out loud also helps. Then burn the piece of paper.

Praying recognizes that we need the Lord's help in this matter. Although silent prayers register with the Lord, it is best for our own assurance to call out audibly, "Lord, help me to remember and renounce rash promises that I have made."

ENDNOTES ON CHAPTER 12

Jesus told a parable about a rich man who planned to store up a bountiful harvest so that he could retire in luxury. But he died that very night. (Luke 12:16–21. I quoted part of verse 19 and all of verse 20.)

The apostle Paul wrote, "Be not deceived; God is not mocked: for whatsoever a man soweth, that shall he also reap" (Gal. 6:7).

Jesus, when saying that it is wrong to judge, warned that judgements can come back on the person judging. (Matt. 7:1–2)

"Whatever is worth doing at all, is worth doing well," is a saying first written in 1774 by Philip Stanhope, 4th Earl of Chesterfield, in a letter to his son.

Moses' directive about repenting for making a rash vow is found in Leviticus 5, verses 4 to 6.

Shakespeare's Hamlet said, "Assume a virtue, if you have it not."

The apostle Paul wrote, "For all the law is fulfilled in one word, even in this; Thou shalt love thy neighbour as thyself" (Gal. 5:14).

"Let love be without dissimulation" (part of Rom. 12:9).

A religious leader asked Jesus which was the greatest commandment.

> Jesus said unto him, Thou shalt love the Lord thy God with all thy heart, and with all thy soul, and with all thy mind. This is the first and great commandment.
>
> And the second is like unto it, thou shalt love thy neighbour as thyself (Matt. 22:37–39).

In the Gospel According to Mark, Jesus' response is slightly different.

> And Jesus answered him, The first of all the commandments is, Hear, O Israel; The Lord our God is one Lord: And thou shalt love the Lord thy God with all thy heart, and with all thy soul, and with all thy mind, and with all thy strength: this is the first commandment.
>
> And the second is like, namely this, Thou shalt love thy neighbour as thyself. There is none other commandment greater than these (Mark 12:29–31).

For the first commandment, Jesus was referring to Deuteronomy 6, verses 4 and 5. The law of Moses about loving our neighbour is found in Leviticus 19, verse 18.

Printed in the United States
by Baker & Taylor Publisher Services